CALL Essentials
Principles and Practice in CALL Classrooms

Joy Egbert

Typeset in Adobe Garamond and Syntax.
by Capitol Communication Systems, Inc., Crofton, Maryland USA
and printed by Victor Graphics, Inc., Baltimore, Maryland USA
Indexed by Coughlin Indexing Services, Annapolis, Maryland USA

Teachers of English to Speakers of Other Languages, Inc.
700 South Washington Street, Suite 200
Alexandria, Virginia 22314 USA
Tel 703-836-0774 • Fax 703-836-6447 • E-mail publications@tesol.org •
http://www.tesol.org/

Director of Publishing: Paul Gibbs
Managing Editor: Marilyn Kupetz
Copy Editor: Craig Triplett
Additional Reader: Sarah Duffy
Cover Design: Capitol Communication Systems, Inc.

Figure 2.1. Copyright © 2000 by Tim Johns. Used with permission.
Figure 3.1. Copyright © 1996 by Adam Rado. All rights reserved. Used with permission.
Figure 3.2. Copyright © Tom Snyder Productions, Inc. Used with permission.
Figure 4.1. Photo taken by author.
Figure 4.2. College of Education, Washington State University. Used by permission.
Figure 5.1. Mark Twain photo by www.PDImages.com.
Figure 5.2. "Janet" used with permission of Right Seat Software, Inc., publisher of Vox Proxy.
Figure 6.1. The NASA SCIence Files-A, NASA Langley Research Center. Produced by the
Office of Education's Distance Learning Center.
Figure 8.1. Copyright © 2004 by FableVision. Used with permission.
Figure 9.1. Screenshot of 21st Century Literacies: Tools for Reading the World reprinted by
permission. Copyright © 1999 by Debbie Abilock, NoodleTeach: NoodleTools, Inc., http://
www.noodletools.com/debbie/literacies/21c.html
Figure 9.2. Copyright © 1994 by Larry Magid. Used with permission.
Figure 10.1. Copyright © 1997 by Learning Point Associates. All rights reserved. Used with
permission.
Figure 11.1. Used with permission of Dell Computers, Inc.

Thanks to Lee Ehman at Indiana University for permission to use his Mystery Character activity.

Thanks also to the teachers who contributed their thoughts to the Teachers' Voices section in
each chapter.

Every effort has been made to contact the copyright holders for permission to reprint borrowed
material. TESOL regrets any oversights that may have occurred and will rectify them in future
printings of this work.

ISBN 1931185158
LCCN 2004097288

▶ This book is for my favorite buddies—I'm glad you're home.

Table of Contents

▶ Preface

A popular *Calvin and Hobbes* comic strip that I often use in my technology classes focuses on an idea I find central to classroom technology use. In the strip, the little boy Calvin is talking to his dad. The conversation goes like this:

Calvin: If I had a computer, I'm sure I'd get better grades on my book reports.

Dad: You'd still have to read the book and tell the computer what you want to say, you know.

Calvin: Man, what's all the fuss about computers? (Watterson, 1995)

Although this comic was published almost 10 years ago, the question that Calvin poses is one that language educators must still ask. I hope that this book shows in part what the fuss should be about.

▶ Purposes

During the years since I co-edited *CALL Environments* (Egbert & Hanson-Smith, 1999), I, along with the field of computer-assisted language learning (CALL), have grown and changed. This book is the result of some of those changes. My intent is to follow my own good advice in earlier works and place pedagogical goals first. Therefore, in devising this book, I have assumed that good teachers teach well because they bear in mind certain principles about how they can best help learners to learn language. Placing these principles at the center of attention makes it much easier for teachers to concentrate on the question of what constitutes effective computer-enhanced pedagogy and why.

Like *CALL Environments,* this book takes as its organizing principle conditions that are known to support effective language learning; however, rather than treating these conditions as discrete entities, I approach them more appropriately as a system upon which effective pedagogy can be built. Examples throughout the book underscore the need to consider the conditions as a whole in every aspect of the teaching and learning process. Some of the points in this book I have made in other places; much of the content I discovered during the writing process. All told, it provides an accurate picture of what CALL classrooms can be like today. Of course, that could change tomorrow.

▶ Organization and Content

In this book I discuss what I have found to be essential to effective CALL. Therefore, I have not included software or hardware how-tos and I have tried not to duplicate what I have seen in other excellent texts on CALL. The emphasis on Web- and Internet-based resources reflects these tools' growing influence around the world. The content of each chapter includes a scenario that helps readers envision the principles at work. After each scenario I briefly cite research in fields such as language acquisition, educational technology, and CALL to build a foundation for chapter activities. The research is explained and explored in a manner appropriate to a practitioner audience. I then present tips and techniques for teachers to consider in developing CALL activities. I do not speak to one specific teaching method or technique because there is as yet no one best way; those following philosophies as different as behaviorism and constructivism can use these basic ideas about what's essential for effective CALL. Chapters provide examples for English language contexts (ESL/EFL K–adult) and content areas, but many of the ideas and principles can be applied easily to teaching other languages and content. I hope particularly that content-area (mainstream) teachers will be able to use the principles and activities with all of their students. In addition, activities and ideas overlap throughout the book, demonstrating that it is not just the technology or the language that is important, but a whole learning environment system that teachers can create with their students.

The introductory chapter defines CALL and presents the principles and guidelines on which to build CALL practice. The first part of the book (chapters 2–3) presents ways that using computers can enhance skill learning and practice, and the second part (chapters 4–6) takes a more holistic view of

CALL as it presents complementary activities for problem solving, collaboration, communication, and production. Chapters 7–10 examine other issues in CALL such as content-based teaching, teacher development, assessment, and limitations. The concluding chapter presents tools and ideas that I have found particularly useful in studying about and using technology in language education. The examples presented throughout the book span language modes, content areas, and student language levels, and they are built on the belief that language works through real activities.

Resources at the end of the book build on ideas expressed within the chapter and provide additional opportunities for teachers and learners to build effective language learning environments. I have concluded each chapter with a section called "Teachers' Voices." These comments, used with permission, are taken from input by ESL and content teachers in CALL teacher education classes, in e-mail conversations, and in other forums where critical reflection about using technology in language learning and teaching continues.

▶ References

Egbert, J., & Hanson-Smith, E. (Eds.). (1999). *CALL environments: Research, practice, and critical issues.* Alexandria, VA: TESOL.

Watterson, B. (1995). *Calvin and Hobbes tenth anniversary book.* Kansas City, MO: Andrews & McMeel.

Acknowledgments

This book would not exist in its current form without the support and insight of Gina Petrie and Yu-Feng (Diana) Yang and the administrative talents of Lioudmila Trouteva, Ching-Yi (Judy) Tseng, and Jennie Booker. I am indebted to them for their patience, time, and effort. Marilyn Kupetz, the managing editor of TESOL, planted the seed for this book a long time ago and has been supportive throughout the process (including providing chocolate at crucial moments). To the students who had to bear the first drafts, and colleagues like ChinChi Chao who provided comments, I thank you. Thanks also to the publishers and Web masters who gave permission to use screen shots of their work. I would most like to thank the teachers who not only spoke up but also contributed their voices to this book: Adrian Advincula, Erika Barrom, Tobi Beehler, Jennie Booker, April Dalrymple, Henry Drinkwine, Andrea Furniss, Susan Garrison, Michael Hannigan, Jimmie Harter, Gabriela Navarro-Rangel, Colleen Nohl, Tricia Robinson, Jean Sheckler, Martin Sorom, Stephanie Teel, Patty Trovato, Maria Venero, Richelle Vining, Jane Watson, and Sally Wells; I hope to hear more from you.

chapter *1*

▶ Introduction: Principles of CALL

▶ Focus

In this chapter you will

- reflect on definitions of CALL
- learn about conditions for optimal language learning and standards for language teaching
- discover guidelines for using educational technology
- reflect on how the learning environment functions as a framework for CALL practice

▶ Defining CALL

Which of these are examples of computer-assisted language learning (CALL)?

- high school Spanish learners e-mailing college Spanish learners in Spanish
- teams of elementary school students doing a vocabulary matching exercise on the computer
- Malaysian students using a self-access computer lab to complete software-based spelling activities in English
- teachers creating multilingual Web pages so that the parents of their ESL learners will understand what is happening in class
- a Russian language teacher explaining a grammar point using presentation software

If you say they are all examples of CALL, you are right. What exactly is computer-assisted language learning? Basically, it means using computers to support language teaching and learning in some way. This definition applies to all languages, skill areas, and contents. Very specifically, CALL is *software tools* designed to promote language learning (ICT4LT, 2001), but CALL can be looked at in broader ways, too. Levy (1997) describes CALL as a *field* that covers "the search for and study of applications of the computer in language teaching and learning" (p. 1). In an earlier volume, Elizabeth Hanson-Smith and I (Egbert & Hanson-Smith, 1999) characterized the basis of CALL as optimal, technology-enhanced *language teaching and learning environments;* that is, language and content settings in which technology was used as effectively as possible to support learning.

Educators regularly introduce new terms to describe CALL, demonstrating that they are still exploring its boundaries and clarifying its components. Recent labels include *computer-enhanced language learning* (CELL), the more general *technology-enhanced language learning* (TELL), and specific applications such as *computer-based language testing* (CBLT) and *computer-supported reading instruction* (CRI). There are other ways to look at CALL, too. It began as software run on mainframe computers to provide learners with drills and other language practice. Since then, CALL has come to include many different technologies: laptop computers, personal digital assistants (PDAs), digital audio recorders, modem and cable Internet access, local area networking, and more. It has expanded to include using individual drill software as well as using the Internet as a medium to support native and nonnative speaker interaction. Trying to reflect these changes and additions in one definition is an enormous task.

Some authors have attempted to explain CALL by dividing its processes and software packages into categories. For example, some have described CALL according to what students do (fill in the blanks, text manipulation, tutorials, word processing), some according to the skills that it addresses (listening software, reading software), others by where it is used (home, office, school, lab), and yet others by the philosophy that underlies its construction (e.g., Warschauer, 1996, who categorizes it as behaviorist, communicative, or integrative). Each of these definitions and categorizations is useful and correct in its own way. Fortunately, in this confusing assortment of terms and tools, three themes emerge:

1. CALL is focused not on technology but on language learning. The words *enhanced* or *assisted* indicate that technology only facilitates the language learning process. Educators need to avoid putting technology ahead of learning in their classrooms (in other words, educators should not be *technocentric* in their thinking). A more accurate term for using technology in language learning might be *language learning through technology*, reflecting the true position of language in such activity.
2. CALL occurs in many contexts and with many diverse participants. Therefore, practitioners need to be prepared to meet a variety of needs.
3. CALL pedagogy should be grounded in theory and practice from a number of fields, especially applied linguistics, second language acquisition, psychology, and computer science.

Why so much fuss over defining CALL? Like the computer, the book and the chalkboard are important tools in language learning classrooms, but educators do not hear about *book-enhanced language learning* or *chalkboard-enhanced language learning*. However, when these tools were first introduced, they also caused controversy. Books, for example, were thought to damage memory. It is only natural that a tool as new, complicated, and powerful as the computer would cause an even bigger fuss. When teachers and learners have accepted computers as just another learning tool, as they have accepted the book, practitioners in the field will worry far less about how to define CALL. In the meantime, I will define CALL with a set of practical guidelines to help teachers and learners understand and implement CALL in language classrooms.

▶ Research in CALL

Although CALL has been an acknowledged field for many years, research that specifically addresses CALL issues has only begun to take on the rigor and effectiveness that both teachers and researchers need. Educators' views of what CALL is and what it should be have evolved, and researchers have developed new research designs and methods that allow them to investigate complex environments that include technology. Much of the research to date is anecdotal; it consists of narratives from teachers, students, and other stakeholders about what happens in CALL environments. Researchers have also conducted empirical studies of individual tools or discrete language items, but many have commented that applying this type of research to CALL classrooms is problematic (see, e.g., Egbert & Petrie, 2005). Although the benefits of using technology in language classrooms have been widely accepted (Lui, Moore, Graham, & Lee, 2003), the literature reveals that technology does not enhance language learning across contexts as much as it inspires positive attitudes toward technology in those who use it. (For excellent overviews of previous research studies, see Basena & Jamieson, 1996, and Liu et al., 2003.) CALL research is filling these gaps. In the meantime, CALL educators can employ research-based conditions, standards, and principles as they work to use computers as effectively and efficiently as possible in language classrooms.

▶ Principles of CALL

Using technology to support language learning comprises four components:

1. the conditions that help create optimal classroom language learning environments
2. the national ESL standards (Teachers of English to Speakers of Other Languages, [TESOL], 1997) that they support
3. guidelines for technology use in educational settings
4. the National Educational Technology Standards (NETS; International Society for Technology in Education [ISTE], 2002b) for technology learning

Conditions for Classroom Language Learning

Any language lesson should support conditions for optimal classroom language learning environments regardless of the tools used. These conditions, based on research from a variety of literatures, have been characterized in different ways, but a general list (Egbert & Hanson-Smith, 1999) includes the following eight items.

1. **Learners have opportunities to interact socially and negotiate meaning.**
    Although individual practice (e.g., in homework) may help learners master certain elements of structure, more effective learning takes place when learners can use language actively and creatively with people they come to understand. Anyone who has struggled to learn a foreign language has probably had the experience of successfully completing grammar exercises but then being totally tongue-tied when trying to form a simple request in the target language. To prepare learners to perform in authentic settings, they must be allowed to practice in social settings.

2. **Learners interact in the target language with an authentic audience.**
    Learners often have difficulty paying attention when a peer is giving a presentation in class because the information is really addressed to the teacher. They will learn more effectively if they have a stake in what other learners are presenting so that (a) learners interact with each other and (b) learners have a reason to listen and respond. During initial language experiences, negotiation with other language learners in the target language may be at precisely the right level for the struggling student. In more advanced stages of learning, students must have access to sympathetic fluent speakers who are willing to adjust their language to the students' ability.

3. **Learners are involved in authentic tasks.**
    Developing authentic tasks is the most important learning condition because the task influences all of the others. For our purposes, an *authentic task* is one that learners perceive they will use outside of class in their real world or that parallels or replicates real functions beyond the classroom. Even the much maligned grammar drill and practice can be an authentic task if learners see it as enabling them to use language outside of the classroom. A teacher can shout "listen to me, listen to me" to try to get students to pay attention and learn (I have seen this happen), but giving students an interesting, active task that they have the skill, support, and time to complete is more effective. The right task will motivate them and get their attention.

4. **Learners are exposed to and encouraged to produce varied and creative language.**

    Remember having essay anxiety? Being nervous about speaking in front of the class? Picking "C" for all the multiple choice questions you really did know the answers to but would have stated in a different way? Not everyone acquires or can demonstrate knowledge and experience in the same way; this is especially true for learners from different educational and cultural backgrounds. Learners therefore need multiple forms of input and a variety of ways to express themselves as they try on a different language and culture and possibly even a new way of approaching knowledge and the learning process.

5. **Learners have enough time and feedback.**

    Some students work more slowly than others, and some need more or less guidance for different tasks. Giving students the right amount of time and administering appropriate feedback are among the most difficult but also most important conditions to meet.

6. **Learners are guided to attend mindfully to the learning process.**

    All too often, students are told what to learn but not how to learn it. Although each student tends to rely on his or her own particular habits or preferences in learning style, they can learn new ones. Optimal learning, then, is also about how to learn more effectively. Students who perceive a task's *how* and *why* will also be more attentive and more motivated to learn.

7. **Learners work in an atmosphere with an ideal stress/anxiety level.**

    The amount of stress or pressure that helps students learn effectively is different for each person. Language learners should feel comfortable enough to take risks with the target language, but they should not be put to sleep by overly simple-minded tasks and exercises. Educators can create optimal stress (*eustress* or good stress) by matching the degree of difficulty, or challenge, to the students' skills (Cziksentmihalyi, 1990), giving them enough difficulty to keep their attention while providing them with tasks that are possible to complete.

8. **Learner autonomy is supported.**

    Many language classes push learners along a rigid schedule requiring a certain number of book chapters, exercises, and essays in a given amount of time. This teacher-directed syllabus may be effective for some students, but it may ignore the needs of others. Allowing learners to control some facets of their learning can help the teacher to provide for different language levels, interests, and learning styles. For example, learners can choose their own books to read, create their own composition topics, or even choose what kind of tasks they will do and when. Some schools, the University of Oregon English Language Institute, for example, have even used completely individualized learning contracts. Teachers assist students in defining and refining their learning goals and in assessing their own progress (Averill, Chambers, & Dantas-Whitney, 2000).

These eight conditions, which work as a system, support TESOL's pre-K–12 (TESOL, 1997) and adult ESL standards (TESOL, 2003). TESOL is an international professional organization for teachers of English as a second or foreign language.

Integrating ESL Standards

ESL Standards for Pre-K–12 Students (TESOL, 1997) suggest that language learners should be able to communicate effectively in social and academic settings and that they should also learn ways to continue their learning beyond the school setting. The standards, like the conditions just stated, encourage language learning tasks that provide opportunities for students to interact socially in the target language for a variety of purposes.

These standards and conditions can be implemented using many different techniques and tools, for example,

- letting students play roles that encourage active learning
- providing a variety of opportunities for learners to interact with native English speakers
- focusing on language use instead of language study
- using higher order thinking skills
- employing different media
- encouraging meaningful language use
- providing flexible timing for tasks
- promoting a variety of sources of feedback and prompting, including other students
- offering adequate information or research resources
- seizing upon opportunities to assist learners in making crucial choices in the learning process

The TESOL standards present goals for students, and the eight conditions describe classroom learning environments in which those goals might be met.

Both require learners to participate in meeting their own language needs. Computer technologies can assist learners working toward these goals within environments that support their learning.

Meeting Learning Conditions With Computer Support

Computer technologies can help teachers create optimal learning environments in many contexts, but when planning computer-enhanced language learning activities, teachers must put learning goals ahead of technology. As you read the following real-life example, note how the project meets the conditions and standards for language learning.

Example 1

▶ In developing a systems analysis and design project for precollege international students in an intensive English program (see Egbert & Jessup, 2000), the teacher focused on students' interests (they were college-bound business majors), their needs (to learn the vocabulary and culture of U.S. business, to work on all four language skills), and their abilities (academic language competence ranging from intermediate to advanced*). The students were asked to build Web pages for organizations in the community. They had the opportunity to choose a client from among several that the teacher had lined up ahead of time or to find one themselves. During the project, learners received language input through activities such as participating in interviews with their clients, reviewing Web pages of organizations similar to their clients', talking with their teams and their class, and listening to technology lectures. Learner teams interacted with their native-English-speaking clients at least three times—during an initial interview about the organization, an interview after the initial page development, and a final review after the project was completed. The teacher organized the teams and provided a loose structure for the activity, but learners controlled their work process and the design of their Web pages. The teacher also led workshops for the project's technical

*For level definitions, see *ESL Standards for Pre-K–12 Students* (TESOL, 1997).

> aspects and provided support for learning difficult concepts, vocabulary, and skills. The teacher and the class provided feedback on the initial designs and the completed projects. Throughout the project, learners used language for activities such as summarizing their interviews, preparing graphic layouts, and compiling a final portfolio of their projects.

This computer-enhanced language learning project met the conditions for language learning in many ways. The task provided useful skills, content, and contacts for learners in an authentic, real-world setting. Learners interacted with peers and with native English speakers who were an authentic audience because they, too, had a stake in the outcomes. Learners had many different ways to express themselves and many sources of language input—listening, speaking, reading, writing text, and creating graphics. They worked with flexible timelines, technical support, and comprehensible feedback from clients, peers, and the teacher. Furthermore, the task provided a number of opportunities for learners to make choices, and they always had a reason to listen to each other. In addition to meeting the conditions for effective language learning, Example 1 also demonstrates appropriate uses of technology in language teaching and learning.

Example 2

> ▶ Learners in an elementary school in an EFL setting were working in small groups studying vocabulary that they had to know for a quiz. Rather than having them memorize the spelling and definitions of the words by recitation, as they usually did, the instructor had taught the students to use *Puzzle Power* (Version 1.0). The students used the software to create word puzzles they could use to practice the focus vocabulary. Although crosswords were the most popular, the students also felt that the anagrams and Kriss Kross puzzles that their classmates had made were helpful for learning vocabulary.

Instructors may not be able to choose their students' goals, but they often have wiggle room in how these goals are met. In the setting described in Example 2, while using the software and the products of their computer work, the students were thinking intensively about the vocabulary, working for an authentic audience (their classmates), interacting socially, and receiving feedback from peers and the teacher. Students also had choices about which puzzle type to make and how they would define the vocabulary words. This simple change in the way this task was structured made vocabulary learning more fun and motivating for the students and it proved an effective language experience.

Guidelines for Using Educational Technology in Language Classrooms

Providing learners with optimal learning conditions and opportunities to meet the ESL standards for language learning is crucial to CALL, but it is only part of the process. When designing instruction for CALL contexts, teachers must also consider how to use technology so that it supports effective learning. The five guidelines described below, compiled and summarized from the educational technology literature, are similar to those for general educational technology and mainstream classroom settings, but they may be applied differently in language learning contexts. Computer support that is considered effective in the language classroom may differ considerably from that in a music or history classroom, where language is not the focus. Nonetheless, all of these guidelines are important components in any classroom where language is central.

1. **Use technology to support the pedagogical goals of the class and curriculum.**
   Teachers using computer labs are often assigned a specific day and time that their class will use the lab, regardless of whether it fits into the teachers' current learning plan. Admittedly, administrators have a duty to make sure that resources are distributed fairly and that they are used as much as possible, but they are often less concerned with how well the technology supports learning. Rather than designing instruction to use the technology and to learn technology skills (a technocentric approach), the technology use must be subordinated to the learning goals. In other words, teachers should not use the computer simply for its own sake.

2. **Make the technology accessible to all learners.**
   Because learners are individuals, CALL activities should address more than one type of intelligence and more than one style of learning (see Gardner, 1993; Reid, 1997). The technology should be used to address the learners' needs and be useful for a variety of instructional purposes. For example, some students prefer visual activities and others prefer

verbal ones; hence, technology that allows learners to choose whether information is presented through pictures or written text would meet more students' needs than technology that does not offer learners a choice.

3. **Use the technology as a tool.**

Computers are often said to play at least three roles in the classroom: tutor, teacher, and tool (Levy, 1997). The computer as tutor presents drills and practice, usually with some explanatory rules. This role is useful in some cases because remediation and more practice have been shown to improve some students' proficiency. However, drill and practice alone has not been shown to increase language learning. The computer cannot actually serve as a teacher, either, because it is not intelligent or capable of individualized, creative feedback. Turing (1950) suggested that a computer could be deemed intelligent if it could fool someone into thinking that a person rather than a machine were responding when it is asked questions. (This is known as the *Turing test;* technology that passes this test is not yet available in schools.) The most useful way to look at technology is as a tool that supports learning in a wide variety of ways.

4. **Use technology effectively.**

Effective means that students learn language better or faster using the technology than they would have using the tools that would ordinarily be available. Even in the mundane area of grammar drills, for example, the classroom teacher can provide a limited amount of feedback to each learner because only one student at a time can answer a grammar practice exercise and receive the teacher's assessment. By using a grammar software package in the computer lab, however, each student can obtain instant and appropriate (although not creative) feedback. In this case, the grammar software might provide more effective grammar practice than the teacher could in the classroom. CALL technology can perform functions previously undreamt of in the classroom, which is why CALL users are so enthusiastic about it.

5. **Use technology efficiently.**

Efficient indicates that technology accomplishes learning goals with less time and work for teachers and learners. For example, a listening program on a computer can instantly replay a passage while an older technology, such as the audio tape, may waste the students' time because it requires rewinding and hunting for the right segment many times.

Another example is simulation software that enables the computer to keep track of thousands of calculations that affect the outcomes. Using this software, the learner can focus solely on the language and content, while, in the background, the computer remembers scores, locations on the screen, turn taking, timing, and so on.

Language teachers designing CALL lessons should consider these guidelines; how these guidelines play out, however, will differ according to not only the course's content, but also to other contextual features such as grade level, student proficiency level, and curricular goals.

Completing a WebQuest (Dodge, 1998) is one effective way to use the computer for language learners across contexts. It uses two of the most powerful electronic tools currently available: the Internet and the word processor. A WebQuest is an inquiry-based task that uses authentic Web and non-Web resources to transform knowledge in some way. Each learner has one or more roles and is actively receiving and using language throughout the task. Example 3 shows how a group project can enable all learners to participate.

Example 3

> ▶ In Cohee's (n.d.) *Wandering the World WebQuest* for ESL students, learners are placed in teams and asked to develop an itinerary for a trip with their teammates. They are to prepare travel plans for New Delhi, Mexico City, and Beijing. Within each group, one member is responsible for figuring out what to pack, one for deciding how much and what kind of money they will need, and the third for choosing interesting tourist sites. Combining all the information they find, team members negotiate the order in which they will visit these destinations, what they will pack, how much money they will take, and what they will see. After completing their itinerary, teams write postcards home from each place they "visit."

In this example, learners are immersed in the language throughout the task; the Web sites they visit on the Internet will be written in the target language and will provide both textual and graphical support (and possibly also musical enhancement) for students with different learning preferences and abilities. Students negotiate meaning with their teammates while solving a problem, in this case, seeking information and organizing it into an itinerary. They communicate and receive language input both orally, as they compile team information, and in written form, as they write their postcards. In addition, giving each team member a different role to play will keep learners constantly on task. The students have easy access to information and can interact immediately with an authentic audience appropriate for their experiences and language level. Using these technology tools is appropriately efficient and highly motivating in ways that book research using pencil and paper cannot match. Under these conditions, using CALL would likely enable effective language and content learning.

Integrating the National Educational Technology Standards

Although using technology as a tool can help our language learners to achieve, it can also help them to meet many of the ISTE's (2002b) NETS for technology-literate students. The NETS were developed to assist educators in "establishing enriched learning environments supported by technology" (ISTE, 2002b). CALL educators share this goal. Upon leaving school, the NETS require that students will be able to

- use a computer and peripherals
- practice responsible use of technology
- use electronic resources appropriately
- design, develop, and publish products
- gather information
- collaborate with others

These standards fit together nicely with the TESOL standards, technology guidelines, and learning conditions already noted. For example, the TESOL standards and the conditions suggest that students use different kinds of media in their learning, and the NETS advise students to use a computer and peripherals, which provide access to a variety of media. In addition, the TESOL standards recommend that students learn to use language and pragmatics appropriately—which might also meet the NETS of using resources appropriately and responsibly. The NETS goals of publishing, gathering information, and collaborating provide language learners with effective opportunities to learn language as described by the conditions and the TESOL standards.

► Conclusion

Standards, guidelines, criteria, definitions—it seems that teachers have much to think about. However, the conditions, standards, and guidelines overlap, which suggests that using technology for language learning relies on certain fundamental principles and that choosing one set of standards, conditions, or guidelines as a foundation for designing a CALL activity might help teachers to meet many of the others. In this text, the eight language learning conditions form the framework for discussions of both theory and practice, reflecting the belief that CALL should focus on language learning. For easier reference, these conditions will be referred to throughout the text as

- interaction
- authentic audience
- authentic task
- production and exposure
- time and feedback
- intentional cognition
- atmosphere
- autonomy

These conditions are described in more detail throughout the book, and tips and techniques to help teachers meet these conditions are discussed in each chapter. Where appropriate, discussions will also mention relevant standards and guidelines to demonstrate clearly how these principles can be applied to CALL thinking and practice. Just as in any classroom, these conditions, standards, and principles are essential for ensuring that using technology in language classrooms always facilitates learning.

► Teachers' Voices

The fact is, technology does mess up and sometimes my whole lesson goes down the drain because things aren't working the way they should. I think you have to be aware and have a back-up plan in the beginning . . . what will I do if things don't go as planned? I'm amazed how flexible my students can be and how willing to try . . . [and] try again.

I think one of the reasons I have felt overwhelmed with the use of technology in the classroom is that I would think about how to use the technology versus how to best integrate technology into the learning process. By starting first with the goal or standard I want my students to master and demonstrate their learning, I can now better see how to integrate a variety of methods to teach the concepts, and for students to demonstrate what they learn, technology being one of the methods.

The ISTE standards are very comprehensive. I am surprised that more schools are not familiar with them. When my husband was involved in hiring an interim technology teacher, I suggested that he ask the candidates about the ISTE standards. He received many blank stares from candidates for the position. We are using the ISTE standards in our school/district to create grade-level proficiency goals for technology. Unfortunately, technology goals are often tacked on rather than infused into content-area curriculum goals. While there are specific technology goals established by a technology committee, there needs to be ownership over who will be responsible for addressing these goals.

When deciding whether or not to use software, I think it is important to evaluate if technology would be better than other methods, such as hiring an aid to help the students or having native English speakers work with English language learners. I do realize that technology is a wonderful creation, but not all students work best with a computer screen.

I think that technology provides another medium for students to express themselves—by showing their work or interacting with concepts/content through the computer. For those students who aren't solely auditory or visual learners, they can go to a computer and often engage in multiple forms of intelligence and learning styles (through multimedia).

Maybe you can help answer this question for me. In the chapter, one of the principles or guidelines stated that if the computer doesn't support learning, it shouldn't be used just to be used. I completely agreed with this statement as I read it, but later began to reflect upon when it wouldn't be used to support learning. For example, if all students are doing is just playing around on a computer, aren't they still meeting some of the ISTE national standards for technology, by just learning how to operate and work with a computer? True, it would be better if students were also doing something with content or language learning at the same time . . . but, still, even if all they are doing is exploring how a computer works, aren't they still learning something valuable?

I agree that exploration and practice itself is a task that will facilitate future use of the computer for students in general. I believe that teachers will be the ones to guide the children through the process of familiarizing themselves with the "how" and "why" things work. At the same time I agree with Condition number 7 in that "language learners should feel comfortable enough to take risks . . . but they should not be put to sleep by overly simple-minded tasks."

Computer access or no computer access, students first need to know how to ask questions that will get to meaningful answers. Even if we don't have computers for all our students all the time, we can still teach these skills.

You can't force curriculum to relate to a learner's life, but you can use the learner's life to reinforce curriculum.

chapter *2*

▶ Developing and Practicing Reading and Writing Skills

▶ Focus

In this chapter you will

- reflect on the benefits of using computers for reading and writing

- learn techniques and guidelines for developing student reading, writing, and grammar skills

- explore software and Web sites that emphasize student reading, writing, and grammar mastery

As you read the scenario below, think about the impact that using technology can have on student skill learning.

In the computer lab at Franklin Elementary School, Mr. Gilchrist is helping his fifth- and sixth-grade ESL students work independently on developing their reading and writing skills. He has conducted many assessments of and with his students, and he and each of his students have developed goals and tasks for the lab time. Today, Rodrigo, a Spanish-speaking student who has not yet developed English language literacy, is working with the bilingual Spanish-English Usborne's Animated First Thousand Words (n.v.) to learn basic English vocabulary. As he works with the tasks in the program, he notes important words in his vocabulary journal. He will later add these words to his personal English dictionary. Sara, an Iranian student who needs to improve her spelling to meet grade-level targets, is using Spell-It Plus (n.v.). After she takes the quiz at the end of the current unit, she reports her progress to Mr. Gilchrist, and together they make a plan for how she will use her new spelling words in her writing. Oleg, a Russian student, is learning how to use writing strategies by using Starter Paragraph Punch (Version 4.4) to complete a paragraph. Sasha, from Ukraine, and Gisela, from Peru, are working together to improve their writing organization by outlining their cooperative story in Kidspiration (Version 2.0). Danny, a Somali, listens as the computer reads Mercer Mayer's Just Me and My Mom (n.v.) and shows Danny which words it is reading. Other students work on reading pace with Versatext (Version 2.7) and phonics development with Reader Rabbit: Dreamship Tales (Version 1.0). All students in the lab are working individually or in pairs on tasks that will help them meet the skill goals they have set for themselves. Mr. Gilchrist works with individual students who have questions or need extra help, and he makes informal assessment notes in his personal digital assistant (PDA) as he observes the activity in the lab.

▶ Overview of Reading and Writing in Language Learning

Many variables play a role in reading and writing achievement. Among the most important are authentic audience, knowing a first language (Ernst-Slavit & Mulhern, 2003), and schema (Carrell, 1987). Goals for reading and writing include speed, accuracy, and comprehension, and skills include summarizing, understanding the main point, identifying how a reading or writing is organized, evaluating how well a writer supports his or her argument, using strategies to understand unknown vocabulary, generalizing, using sight words, predicting, and drawing conclusions. In writing, the popular 6+1 trait writing framework focuses on content, organization, voice, word choice, sentence fluency, and conventions such as proper spelling and grammar (Northwest Regional Education Laboratory [NWREL], 2001). Most important for skills development is *noticing* (Schmidt, 2001), or focusing attention on the differences between one's own language and the target language.

Other chapters in this text integrate reading, writing, and other language skills and modes for purposes such as communicating, problem-solving, and producing. This chapter focuses on the skills involved in reading and writing and on how to practice those skills using a computer. Although educators are still debating whether skills learning or a whole language approach is more effective, most agree that mixing these approaches is effective for language learning because it addresses a variety of learning styles and focuses on both fluency and accuracy (Freeman & Freeman, 2000; Gibbons, 2002). Language programs vary widely in how they treat language skills, but many programs around the world have a strong skills base. Learners in these and other programs often find grammar and other discrete skill learning an authentic part of language learning.

Regardless of how the balance between the whole and parts plays out in your classroom, if you want to teach reading and writing skills (and the grammar involved in them) to language learners, computer technologies can certainly help. As AlKahtani (1999) notes, computer use can support learning in a number of ways:

> They can check exercises after they are done, move students gradually from easier to more difficult exercises according to their levels and abilities. When students fail to answer questions correctly or perform activities, the computer can simulate, drill or explain the phenomenon. (p. 1)

Although skills software has typically provided uncontextualized, fill-in-the-blank type drills, much has changed in the past decade and more variety in skills learning is available (Higgins, 1993). *Skills tools* currently take many forms and support many activities, as evidenced by this chapter's opening scenario. Newer software programs offer media-rich examples and integrate effective scaffolding to help students understand and retain skills. In addition, hypertext, or text linked nonlinearly to other text, can be seen as a skills tool because it offers learners multiple paths into the text, which Cary (2000) sees as crucial. The vast number of Internet resources is also a major advantage for skills teaching; Web sites and software can provide a variety of easily accessible text types and articles written in numerous genres at a wide range of readability levels.

Access to these technologies can also provide texts and instructions in different languages, helping learners to build literacy foundations in their first languages, and teachers are more likely to find something to pique learners' interest in the wide variety offered online than in the small preselected set of readings offered in printed textbooks. Tools such as these can help to individualize learning, thereby giving students more opportunities to control their learning through what they see as authentic tasks.

▶ Supporting Reading and Writing

The following two instructional techniques support not only reading and writing, but also language learning in general:

1. **Provide opportunities for individualized learning to benefit students at all levels.**
   Encouraging students to work at their own level presents effective challenge and thereby supports the development of skills (Csikszentmihalyi, 1997). Individualized learning does not, however, imply that students should always work alone. The needs of individual students can be provided for in many ways while they work with groups or the whole class. Teachers can begin by assessing student needs in a variety of situations, as Mr. Gilchrist does continually.

2. **Let students, not the tools or texts, determine authenticity.**
   In recent years the second language literature has advocated using authentic materials for teaching, which typically means using materials made for a native-speaking audience. The idea behind using such texts is to motivate students to study and to expose them to real language. However, this definition of authentic materials overlooks an important fact outlined in chapter 1; *authentic* can mean whatever material the students perceive as useful for using the target language outside of class. If students do not believe that a local newspaper (usually considered authentic material) is useful to their lives or their learning, the fact that it was written for a native-speaking audience does not make it authentic to those students.

In the chapter's opening scenario, Mr. Gilchrist's language learners have the opportunity to work on tasks that they chose based on their interaction with the teacher. Although this is difficult to accomplish in large, teacher-fronted classrooms, it is possible when students can receive some of their feedback from computers. Students in Mr. Gilchrist's classroom were motivated because they were working on areas that they found personally relevant (authentic) and challenging.

▶ Tips for Designing Opportunities for Skill Development

Here are two more important tips for designing activities that help students develop reading and writing.

1. Students must be taught learning strategies. This idea is mentioned in other chapters, but here it pertains specifically to skill learning. Strategies such as discerning patterns, using context clues, word analysis, guessing, and deducing are effective at helping learners reach reading and writing goals (Anderson, 2002; Oxford, 1994; for sample lessons, see Goodman, Watson, & Burke, 1996). The use of concordancers (Rosenthal, 2003), or software that reads through texts and lists incidences of chosen words in their context, not only helps English language learners to better understand how to use grammar but can also help them to practice formulating rules from examples (deduction). Figure 2.1 presents an example of concordance data.

2. Students should be exposed to extensive reading and writing. The age-old adage that students learn to read by reading still holds; students can improve their skills through contextualized practice. The Internet can help with this task, for example, by exposing learners to other learners at their levels with whom they can exchange messages and discuss readings, and software-based stories on compact discs (CDs) provide both audio and video exposure to text. Teachers can adapt computer-based materials and texts by adding external documents (Egbert, 2001) that help students notice conventions or by following suggestions to adapt such activities as WebQuests (see, e.g., San Diego State University, 2002).

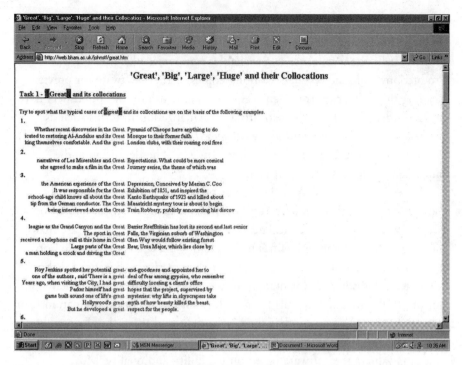

Figure 2.1. Example of concordance data from Johns's (2000) *Data Driven Learning Page.*

▶ Evaluating Web Sites and Software for Reading and Writing

Many of the activities in other chapters throughout this text support reading and writing. These activities also meet many conditions and principles for language learning, including exposure and production. With the incredible number of possible activities, programs, and Web sites, how can teachers choose appropriately? After identifying sites and programs that might help them meet their instructional goals, teachers can follow several steps. First, when using Web sites either as a teacher resource or part of instructional materials, make sure that the site is published by an association or organization that is trustworthy. Many teaching organizations and schools have Web sites with great suggestions, materials, and links. Check to see when the site has been updated, and look through it carefully for biases or other problems. If students will go to the site, make sure that the language level is appropriate or that they will have help if needed. For software, get a full demonstration first. If your school technology leader or a colleague has the program available, ask him or her to model it for you and to explain how they use it. If the software is not available, companies like Tom Snyder Productions will send teachers working copies of their software for preview. Reading the CD jacket is not enough—software authors and publishers have different ideas about what constitutes contextualization in terms such as *grammar in context,* for example, with *context* ranging from individual unlinked sentences to authentic reading passages. The definition and implementation must suit your goals.

Second, after choosing likely sites or programs, teachers should evaluate them as closely as time and effort allow. (If time is an issue, complete one or two per week; share with colleagues; let students do some.) There are many different checklists and guidelines for evaluating these resources, based on cost, structure, technical features, or other characteristics. Because this book advocates using software for many purposes, including some for which it was not originally intended, it calls for a slightly different view of evaluation from other guidelines. Assuming that the cost is right and the technology will work in your school or program, then, like Bradin (1999) in *CALL Environments,* you can evaluate the software based on feasibility and quality. Most important are the following factors:

1. **Goals:** What can the software or Web site do (not what it can't), and how does this meet pedagogical goals?

2. **Presentation:** How does the software do it? (Does it introduce or practice? Is there context? Are there exercises, quizzes, multimedia presentations, something else?) Is this appropriate for the students and goals?

3. **Appropriateness:** How will students be able to use the software to meet goals? (Can students understand it? Does it provide appropriate examples and scaffolds? Is the level appropriate?)

4. **Outcomes:** What do students produce with only the software or Web site? What could students produce with additional documents? What other outcomes are possible?

5. **Evaluation:** What kind of appropriate feedback and evaluation does the software or site offer?

6. **Notes:** Add notes about what else is important to know about the technology for your context. Then balance the results to decide if the software or Web site is useful for your instruction.

This evaluation plan is used in the next section to describe some Web sites and software programs that teachers might consider for reading, writing, and grammar learning and practice.

Web Site Examples

Grammar Safari (D. Mills & A. Salzmann, n.d.)

> ► **Goals:** Help students collect examples of grammar points. Useful for inductive grammar learning.
>
> **Presentation:** Illustrated instructions describe how to use Web browsers to search for terms. It has no preset search items.
>
> **Appropriateness:** This is for intermediate to advanced students who can use inductive reasoning, or who have access to some strategy training. Graphics and layout help with understanding the instructions. Help is provided on how to use browsers and which to use for specific goals.
>
> **Outcomes:** Depends on browser and search—could be a list of the item, a document in which the *find* capability can be used, or an exportable text. Typically not the same as a concordancer.
>
> **Evaluation:** None.

Interlink Language Center Reading Lessons (Interlink Language Centers, n.d.)

> ► **Goals:** Provide practice in extensive reading, speed reading, cloze, reading and listening, and science reading for ESL students.
>
> **Presentation:** Cloze readings have reading on the left and exercises on the right. There is a generous time limit. The readings are taken from real texts. The read-and-listen exercise provides sentence-by-sentence listening and mouse-over definitions of words (they show up in the bar at the bottom of the page).
>
> **Appropriateness:** Students might need initial instructions to understand how to use the site. However, help is provided, navigation is very clear, and the interface is relatively simple.

Readings are presented in different genres, but most are for high intermediate and advanced level students at high school or above.

Outcomes: Quiz-like outcomes only.

Evaluation: When students click on the answer, they are provided with instant feedback that contains an explanation. They are also told which questions they have yet to answer.

Notes: This site also has grammar, writing, vocabulary, and spelling sections. Students could use it independently once they understood the basic instructions. New exercises are added frequently.

PIZZAZ: People Interested in Zippy and ZAny Zcribbling (Opp-Beckman, 2003)

▶ **Goals:** "PIZZAZ! is dedicated to providing simple creative writing and oral storytelling activities with copyable (yes, copyable!) handouts for use with students of all ages" (Opp-Beckman, 2003, ¶1).

Presentation: There are five categories: Poetry, Fiction, Bag of Tricks, More Publishing Opportunities, and Other Teacher Resources. Each section has many links that have complete lessons with student handouts. Some have related links with activities that can be completed online.

Appropriateness: Most of the site is not addressed to students, but some parts are. Navigation is very clear, and language is simple and clear. Useful for many ages and language levels.

Outcomes: The site said that publishing online was possible, but I did not see how.

Evaluation: None—depends on instructor.

Notes: Lessons are simple to read and have many scaffolds, such as examples and outlines, so that learners could teach them to each other.

Word Games (East of the Web, 2002)

▶ **Goals:** Word practice that is not specifically for ESL students but is useful for them as well as native speakers.

Presentation: There are eight word games: Popword, Popword Multi-Player, Wordsearch, Eight Letters, Cryptoquote, Definetime, Storyman, and Codeword. Most focus on predicting letters, finding words or letters among others, and knowledge of vocabulary.

Appropriateness: Some of the words are esoteric, which might frustrate students. Some of the games, like Popword, could be useful for a variety of levels and ages.

Outcomes: Scores.

Evaluation: Typically "wrong, try again" type with no feedback.

Notes: Absolutely addictive, especially Popword. Students would play forever! Need external document for students to record their words or otherwise work with the vocabulary and rules.

Software Examples

Reading the Classifieds (Egbert, 1994)

▶ **Goals:** Students read for meaning, learn about the classified pages in the newspaper and about using them to look for housing, jobs, and dates. Focus on vocabulary, abbreviations, culture, skimming, scanning.

Presentation: Three sections in linear fashion. Students use the external newspaper to find answers to questions the software poses, answer by clicking a button.

Appropriateness: Humor might be misunderstood or misconstrued. Middle-class white values, although an effort has been made to have the characters show differences. Language is appropriate for high level beginners and above.

Outcomes: It is an action maze-style program, so choices lead to results and other choices. Students either succeed or fail at securing housing and other necessities.

Evaluation: There is no specific feedback, but learners see the consequences of their actions so the results are meaningful.

Notes: This freeware can be copied many times. Students should work individually—not appropriate for groups without some creative adaptation.

Focus on Grammar—Basic (Eckstut, 1998)

▶ **Goals:** Help students understand and practice specific grammar points.

Presentation: There are 15 sections, including one for review. Each section introduces the grammar point (identify and recognize) and provides practice with listening, reading, and writing the point. Listening, for example, includes dictation and recall. The program marks what students have completed so that they know where they left off.

Appropriateness: Ms. Enders' sophomores like this so much they check it out to take home. They feel that it helps them communicate correctly and that it counterbalances the whole approach in their ESL class. It is useful for inductive learners and is meant for adult learners, but high school students could use it, too.

Outcomes: Typically, just answers to the quiz, although in the writing section students can construct paragraphs.

Evaluation: Answers are always available. Right or wrong type, typically with feedback.

Notes: Sentences are uncontextualized—no graphics, mostly word or sentence level—and it provides excellent support (charts, vocabulary definitions, explanations, appendixes).

Imagination Express Destination: Time Trip, USA
(Version 1.1)

▶ **Goals:** "Inspire the reluctant writer." Gain historical insights, learn how history affects everyday life, and support thematic learning. Provide reading for other students, and practice speaking.

Presentation: The scrapbook section presents animation, text, and sound for students to understand time periods. The view section allows students to view precreated books. It presents story ideas orally and in text. Students construct their own books, using graphics, sound, music, text, and animation by clicking (no programming).

Appropriateness: Simple, clear layout makes it easy to navigate. The teachers' guide says K–8, but older learners can enjoy it since it is basically content-free. Text can be written in any language supported by the computer.

Outcomes: A book or other multimedia document.

Evaluation: None within the program.

Notes: Mr. Blackwood says his students like to spend a lot of time choosing graphics, so make text central. It is ideal for group work and presentation as well as historical/cultural content learning. The teacher's guide contains many suggestions, including ESL ideas for expanding vocabulary, answering questions, and demonstrating understanding of text by creating appropriate graphics. It can be used in young child or adult mode.

Reading for Meaning (Version 1.0)

▶ **Goals:** Improve reading comprehension.

Presentation: There are five whole-class model lessons, and then students use it in groups or individually. Topics include main idea, inference, sequence, cause and effect, and compare and contrast. Genres include tall tales, poems, novel excerpts, *National Geographic* excerpts, and more.

Handouts and graphic organizers are included, as are lesson plans for each text presented. The "student picker" randomly chooses students to answer, based on cooperative learning principles. Texts are presented in video, voices, text, and graphics, and printouts are provided for students to read along. Lessons are cooperative and vary in ability level. Lessons have three steps: read, think, and write.

Appropriateness: The teachers' guide says it is for Grades 3–8, but other levels are appropriate depending on interest and ability. It presents characters and writings from different cultures and a wide range of readings.

Outcomes: Graphic organizers, writing handouts.

Evaluation: Answers are provided. Students must also assess their answers and their process.

Notes: It is fun, and it provides ample scaffolding for teachers and students. It is written for native speakers, but it is so diverse and well constructed that it can be used for second language learners without much adaptation.

A notebook or electronic file with entries like the ones shown in the examples can provide teachers with ideas for a variety of lessons and a record of technologies that they have reviewed.

▶ More Ideas for CALL Reading and Writing Activities

As Meyers (1993) notes in her wonderful text about multicultural learners, students should not only read and write every day, but they should also have opportunities to share their ideas and writings. One of the strengths of using computers in reading and writing is that electronic technologies can provide forums in which learners can share their work with others. Ideas and resources for students to share work are presented in the resources at the end of this book. Two additional reading and writing activities that computer use can support are journal writing and MOOing.

Journal writing provides students with many clear benefits (Kreeft-Peyton, 1990). It allows students to practice writing, receive modeling, gain authentic input, and communicate with others. Journals can be written among learners, between the teacher and learner, between learners and experts, or even between learners and parents. Learners can write their journals in a first language, additional language, or combination of the two (or more), using academic or informal writing. More broadly, e-mail journals (Goettsch, 2001) can be used to connect with learners in other cities, states, and countries, and to help learners gain insights about different cultures, literatures, and language uses. Because it uses one of the more accessible and simple technologies, learners can use e-mail journaling even in contexts with less advanced technologies.

MOOing, or participating in a text-based electronic world, allows learners to use language not only to communicate, but also to navigate, build, play games, and investigate. *SchMOOze University* (http://schmooze.hunter .cuny.edu/), the first MOO (multi-user object-oriented domain) built specifically for ESL students, is a synchronous environment where learners interact in real time with other learners around the world who are logged on. However, MOOing is not an intuitive activity for most students, and the instructor and the learners must learn how the system works and how to make the best use of it. Backer (2001) suggests that the linguistic benefits are well worth the time expended.

▶ Conclusion

This chapter has presented many ideas and resources for computer-enhanced support of reading and writing. Language learners do not need computers to learn grammar, read with comprehension, or write for an authentic audience. However, teachers can use computers to help them address individual learners' needs, and provide effective, authentic language tasks and texts.

▶ Teachers' Voices

Have you checked out http://www.pbs.org/teachersource? I love the link to *Between the Lions* because it has *Word Play*. English language learners (and beginning students) get to click on the word, see the spelling, hear what it sounds like, and see what it does. Very valuable for English language learners! Other links will also take you to subjects for more advanced students.

I have always thought that drill activities have no value to students and therefore don't like using them, but the author brings up a good point that drill activities can be made into something beneficial by supplementing the drills with external documents like handouts and graphic organizers. Also, you can arrange different roles for your students so your students have the ability to interact when doing the drills and can negotiate meaning with their partner, which is one of the optimal conditions for language learning environments. Now I am aware that drills can be used with learners if supplemented.

Looking through our "library" I found an article by Deborah Healey from Oregon State. She mentioned a software list: TESOL CALL Interest Section Software List. Good info: title, company, price, age level, content area. You can also go to the Oregon State Web page and search for Deborah Healey—there is other info, but look for the TESOL CALL Software List.

I find all this technology important to learning; however, I do not find it more important than understanding how to read (with comprehension) and write (effectively). We are losing the art of penmanship and the ability to use words beautifully. As a high school teacher I would really like to get students who know proper punctuation, grammar, and spelling. For those of us who are old enough to remember, we used to have to rewrite what the teacher had written on the board. This was good for several reasons, one of which is it modeled proper use of the language. I know the technology is cool and that it makes life easier, but does easy always translate into better?

One professor shared with me how one of her students purposely chose not to do well on his assignment. I think this was a huge software package that mostly focused on discrete literacy skills and tests that were leveled. I don't think it was that he really liked the response the computer gave him, but he liked not having to move forward, because this was familiar to him and he had worked the system. It took her a few weeks or even months to figure out that this student was purposely choosing the wrong answers to stay at the same comfortable level.

I really like the idea of using external documents with tutorial-type software. I think it will really expand the use of a lot of the software that is available to us as educators. After reading and thinking about the use of external documents, I can see that I have not been using the software I have available to me very effectively. In the past I have used my drill-type software as something the students can play around with in the morning before school starts, or during any free time they might have. After reading about this, I decided to rework a 20-minute math review block of time I have. I have divided the class into groups, and have one group use the computers with external documents—working at their level—another group works with a para-pro [paraprofessional], and another group works with me with little chalkboards. (We have kind of the mix of old teaching styles with new technology—computers and chalkboard slates!) The external documents keep the accountability up. The students will have a paper to turn in at the end of the week that will show what they have accomplished while working with the software. I wish I had started this at the beginning of the year.

Technology in and of itself may be fun, but in our classrooms, the use of technology needs to support goals and student learning. I can teach to curriculum goals in a variety of ways. When I reach to technology, it is because it will enhance learning. Using a specific piece of software such as Inspiration provides a graphic organizer that helps my students meet a learning objective. For example, I want students to look at many aspects of character development when they are creating a character in a story. If I build a template in Inspiration, in which students define a character in terms of physical characteristics, how the character is viewed by others, how the character changes over time, etc., these are valuable content goals. If I ask students to map these qualities using Inspiration software, they do a more complete analysis of a character. They are drawn to the computer because it is fun to create a web, but they do a more thorough job of character development because they are using software and it's fun. The bottom line is the character development. The use of Inspiration software encourages this development.

Last week I had my students do some Mad Libs online (www.eduplace.com /tales), to work with parts of speech. The collaborative aspect here is that they added to the computer-created outline with their own words. Even better, they could supplement their words in a student-created Mad Lib which had been created by another student their age. If so inclined, each student could then submit their own Mad Lib to the compilation online. They loved printing out their results and trying to think of new stories to submit. We're working on it more this week. The posted Mad Libs were about everything from school lunch to a first date. What do you think?

chapter 3

Developing and Practicing Listening and Speaking Skills

▶ Focus

In this chapter you will

- reflect on the benefits of using computers for listening and speaking

- learn techniques and guidelines for supporting and developing student listening and speaking skills

- explore software and Web sites that emphasize student listening and speaking mastery

As you read the anecdote below, think about how using technology can help students develop listening and speaking skills.

Ms. Ono's Japanese high school English language learners are planning to take a trip from Tokyo to New York City, and they are concerned that they will not be able to speak with native English speakers there. Although they have basic written literacy skills, their listening and speaking abilities are generally poor. Ms. Ono tells them that, although such exercises will not fit into the required curriculum, they may practice in the computer lab after class, and she recommends that they visit *Randall's ESL Cyber Listening Lab* (http://www.esl-lab.com/). There the students find more than 100 listening quizzes ranging in difficulty from easy to very difficult on a wide variety of topics. The quizzes, which feature native English speakers from the United States, contain an audio portion and questions to focus the listening. Students can play them over and over and go up to the next level or topic when they feel that they are ready—they have many choices. Some of the students print the study guide, which helps them to choose the quizzes that are focused on what they want to know. Some of the students work together, discussing the sound bites as they listen; others work industriously by themselves to complete as many quizzes as they can. The Web site provides the correct answers to the students immediately after they answer, and some students go back and listen again to confirm their choices or check where they went wrong. When they just do not understand, they can look at the quiz script and see the words that they are having trouble with, then go back and listen to the audio to hear the pronunciation and use. After several weeks of practice, some of the students begin to feel more confident that they will be able to understand and interact with native speakers when they get to New York.

▶ Overview of Listening and Speaking Skills in Language Learning

To speak and listen fluently and accurately in a second language, language learners need to be able to comprehend and produce—in a native-like fashion—stress, intonation, rhythm, pacing, gestures, and body language, and they need both linguistic and sociolinguistic competence (Florez, 1999). They should understand language functions such as sharing personal narratives, greeting and leave-taking, informing, questioning, clarifying, and interrupting. For practicing and developing skills, Peregoy and Boyle (2001) recommend activities such as singing, role-playing, dramatizing poetry, doing show and tell, tape recording children's books, and choral reading.

Many educators commonly assume that although computer software and the Internet can support student reading and writing effectively, they cannot support student listening and speaking. Whether this is true, however, depends on how these technologies are used. Florez (1999) notes that "opportunities for speaking and listening require structure and planning if they are to support language development" (p. 1), and carefully planned CALL activities can use computers to support listening and speaking. For example, computer technologies can assist students to interact with other English language learners and with native speakers in many different forums not only to practice but also to develop listening and speaking skills. Cary (2000) notes that computers can also "get reluctant speakers to speak English" (p. 36) by providing them with increased opportunities, less teacher fronting, and the authentic and challenging situations that Cary recommends.

Skills tools specifically for language learner listening and speaking take a variety of forms. Like reading and writing skills tools, they are most commonly drill based. However, many other types of tasks and tools can support listening and speaking. Two basic CALL task structures (touched on in chapter 1) promote learner speaking and listening as part of social interaction. Learners can speak *around* the computer, or learners can speak *through* the computer. In addition, some software programs provide learners with opportunities to speak *with* (although not to genuinely interact with) the computer. Each of these structures has different advantages. When designing technology-supported language learning tasks, teachers can use one or more of these structures as appropriate for learners. Examples of these three types of tasks are presented in the following sections.

Listening and Speaking Around the Computer

Learners can work around the computer with learners at their own level to obtain and practice basic skills. They can work with the plethora of listening exercises provided by Web sites such as *The Internet TESL Journal* (see *ESL: Speaking,* 2004; *ESL: Listening,* 2004), *Renata's ESL/CALL Corner* (Setmajer-Chylinski, 2002), or *Dave's ESL Café* (http://www.eslcafe.com/). To listen to the audio, students may have to download a helper program such as RealPlayer (n.v.) or QuickTime (n.v.), but these listening pages provide directions for how to do so. More advanced students can listen to news stories and read the text at the same time at the *National Public Radio* site (http://www.npr.org/) or practice with idioms, pronunciation, spoken grammar and more at *Adam Rado's English Learning Fun Site (ELFS)* (http://www.elfs.com/). Figure 3.1 presents an example from Rado's idioms pages.

These sites benefit students by providing content that enables them to interact with one another; in other words, the listening and speaking that students do around the computer when they talk about the listening and speaking exercises reinforces and provides practice for the concepts under study. To facilitate these Web-based activities, teachers may want to create additional handouts (external documents) that help students interact, understand, and apply what they learn. (For examples of how such external documents work, see Ryan's, 2000, *Recipes for Wired Teachers,* in which many of the lessons use external documents.) External documents can also effectively enhance ESL freeware (cost-free software)—programs that can be downloaded from, for example, *Resources for Teachers of Basic Skills* (Strabu, 1997) or from the *Computer Enhanced Language Instruction Archive* (see LaTrobe University, 2004).

Many content-based software programs written for ESL learners and native speakers have built-in interaction structures that require students to

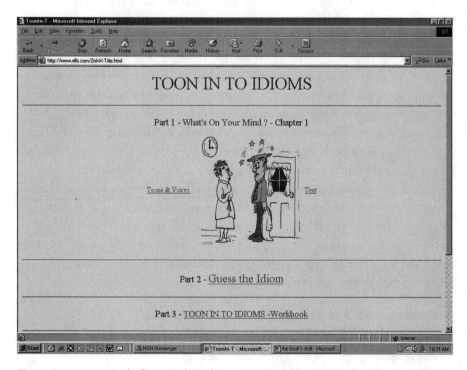

Figure 3.1. An example from Rado's idioms pages on his *ELFS* Web site.

interact around the computer to complete a task. One example is Who Is Oscar Lake? (available from http://www.languagepub.com/; for a walkthrough, see http://www.justadventure.com/), which provides live action video to help learners solve a mystery. Social studies, math, and science programs from companies such as Tom Snyder Productions (http://www.tomsnyder.com/) provide roles and materials with their software products that support oral interaction for learners at all levels using discussion, decision making, and cooperative learning structures.

Working around the computer allows learners to test their language and content hypotheses with peers, to learn pragmatic skills before taking them outside of the classroom, and to have some control over how and when they participate. In these ways, such activities provide opportunities for language learning.

Listening and Speaking Through the Computer

When learners are capable of interacting with more fluent speakers, they can use the computer as a conduit to native speakers and more advanced second language learners around the world. Voice chat and audio e-mail can be modified to work efficiently and effectively for a wide range of classrooms that have access. (One useful and free audio e-mail tool is the consumer version of TalkSender, http://www.talksender.com/.) Activities using both synchronous and asynchronous audio exchanges include audio dialogue journals (see chapter 2 for more on written dialogue journals) in which two or more participants record messages and send them to each other in a running stream of conversation. In addition, learners can practice speaking and listening through the computer by recording audio segments in book-making software or in presentation software such as Microsoft PowerPoint, and they can even trade suggestions for essay revision in versions of Microsoft Word that have audio commenting capabilities. Again, a major benefit of this task structure is that learners can interact socially and receive authentic oral input from peers and others. They also have opportunities to use spoken language with a wide variety of audiences in a safe atmosphere that allows them to record and rerecord until they are satisfied with their results. In these ways, working through the computer enables learners to meet many important language learning conditions.

Listening and Speaking With the Computer

Opportunities for learners to work interactively with the computer on listening and speaking are relatively rare because the computer cannot respond creatively or provide individualized feedback. In addition, speech recognition technologies, although advancing daily, still cannot recognize with complete accuracy the speech of nonnative speakers or even native speakers with strong regional accents. However, several companies provide products that approach this goal, either dictation software or integrated learning systems such as Rosetta Stone (n.v.).

Dictation software packages such as Dragon Naturally Speaking (Version 7.3) and Via Voice (Version 2.01) allow users, once they have trained the software, to speak into a microphone and watch the software type their speech onto a page. Watching the software interpret the learner's speech provides feedback in the mistakes that it reveals in his or her pronunciation and grammar. The user can then instruct the computer orally how to manage the mistakes that it has found.

The Rosetta Stone software models native speaker pronunciation aurally that learners listen to and repeat. Another aspect of the system checks learners' writing after they reproduce a dictated passage. The ELLIS English Language Learning System (Version 3.0), Connected Speech (Version 1.1), and other speaking and listening software packages offer similar features.

As electronic technologies become more advanced, students will be able to work with the computer as a learning partner instead of working around and through it as a tool. For now, however, using the computer as tool provides learners with numerous opportunities to improve their target language listening and speaking skills.

▶ Supporting Listening and Speaking

The following two instructional techniques, which are fundamental to language learning, support listening and speaking.

1. **Provide opportunities for students to notice.**
   Noticing (Schmidt, 2001) is important during reading and writing, as noted in chapter 2, but to produce fluent and comprehensible speech and to react appropriately to the others' speech, students also need to notice their own linguistic errors. Lightbown and Spada (2000) suggest that carefully devised tasks should include providing students access to correct forms that they can discover together.

2. **Include pragmatics in lessons.**
   Teachers can use any of the language modes to teach norms of social appropriateness in the target language culture if they make noticing these features a lesson objective (see Hanford, 2002). For example, video

segments in software can help learners understand body language, gestures, proximity, and other pragmatic functions while they listen. Although communication through the computer such as text and voice chatting can provide only limited pragmatic and sociocultural information, using the computer for these activities is similar pragmatically to using the telephone, another essential skill for many students.

When Ms. Ono in the opening scenario chose *Randall's ESL Cyber Listening Lab* for practice, she picked it because it presents scripts for students to use as scaffolds, allows students to choose the level at which to work, and provides opportunities to replay the audio segments, which helped students notice grammar in native speech. Ms. Ono also wanted the students to have additional practice with the native pace in the audio. These segments were authentic for students because they were planning a trip to the United States; learners might even talk about these very topics on their trip. Although Ms. Ono did not expect that all students would gain in the same ways from using this site, exposing them to it helped prepare them for what they might encounter on their trip.

▶ Tips for Designing Opportunities for Skill Development

In addition to promoting noticing and teaching pragmatics, teachers can help students learn to listen and speak by giving them time to talk to each other every day (Peregoy & Boyle, 2001). Lightbown and Spada (2000) note that although students at the same proficiency level usually cannot correct each other's language mistakes, they do not reproduce each other's mistakes. Rather, peer interaction provides practice in listening, speaking, and negotiating that learners otherwise might not get. Learners can develop speaking, listening, and oral grammar skills through direct instruction or by participating in content or whole tasks, but most important is that learners have opportunities to practice in a variety of authentic venues.

▶ Technologies for Listening and Speaking

Florez (1999) provides a framework for listening and speaking lessons by noting that such lessons "can follow the usual pattern of preparation, presentation, practice, evaluation, and extension" (p. 2). These steps generally include telling students what the goals of the activity are, making sure that they have the skills necessary to perform it, working with the target skill or form, noting learner progress, and following up. Teachers can use this framework to focus the lesson on language learning while integrating technology where it supports language learning most effectively and efficiently. Following are three sample listening and speaking lessons that use this framework and integrate technologies at various points during the lesson to help students learn and practice speaking and listening.

Example 1

▶ **Lesson:** Introducing CALL to Learners

Focus: Interviewing skills, discussion skills, oral summary, question formation, listening for main ideas.

Preparation: Show the learners the computers that they will be using. Ask them to brainstorm what computers are used for. Ask what might be learned with/through computers in a language classroom (i.e., what topics, vocabulary, skills). Type these lists in a word processing or presentation program as the learners participate.

Presentation: Create a survey with learners to find out about previous computer use and skills among members of the class or program. Focus on vocabulary and grammar points as necessary. Work with the class on interviewing skills, model the procedure, and have learners practice with each other.

Practice: Have the learners conduct the survey orally with the target population and take notes on the answers. Learners record all the answers they receive in a simple database.

Evaluation: Based on the answers they received, have learners add to their original list of what computers are used for and what might be learned with/through the technology. Ask students to keep this list and to add to it during the course.

Extension: Have learners, individually or in small groups, survey other language classes. Ask them to report their findings back to the class, and then have the class discuss these findings before entering them into the database.

While working on this lesson, learners are encountering and practicing both pragmatic and linguistic features of the target language. They are meeting learning conditions such as authentic social interaction and production and using technology as a learning tool.

Example 2

▶ **Lesson:** Cultural Debates Online

Focus: Debate/argument skills, discussion skills, presentation skills, question formation, formulating an opinion, asking for clarification, critical thinking skills, pronunciation, using phrases of agreement and disagreement.

Preparation: (a) With learners, brainstorm what culture means and why it is important to its members. Ask learners to reflect on recent or major changes to what they consider their culture. (b) Introduce learners to their e-pals (online pen pals) and have them record oral introductions of their own to send to their e-pals (e.g., using a free audio e-mail package from http://www.etnvoicemail.com/ or using a sound recorder package and attaching the sound file to a regular e-mail message).

Presentation: Learners should read the background information on the Mentawai tribe at *Cultural Debates* (Tom Snyder Productions, n.d.) and discuss it (e.g., compare it to their own culture, develop questions about the culture). They should learn how to pronounce vocabulary and to use forms as needed. Learners then choose one of six possible debates and form small groups based on the debates they chose. Groups view the video associated with their debate and complete the "Consider," "Vote," and "Read" activities on the Web site. They may also use other sources such as electronic and paper encyclopedias, online and off-line books and articles, films, and Web sites to gather additional information to support their argument.

Practice: Learners formulate their arguments in groups and then, at the appointed time, use a synchronous voice chat tool (e.g., Audio-Tips at http://www.audio-tips.com/, PalTalk at http://www.paltalk.com/, or Yahoo! Messenger at http://messenger.yahoo.com/; for download, see Yahoo!, 2002) to discuss their arguments with their e-pals. Learners should take notes during the conversations.

Evaluation: Learners discuss together what they have learned and if any parts of their argument have changed. They then present their argument to the class for additional feedback.

Extension: Learners prepare an entry for their oral journals about what they have learned from this activity and how it has impacted their ideas about their own culture. Or, as the

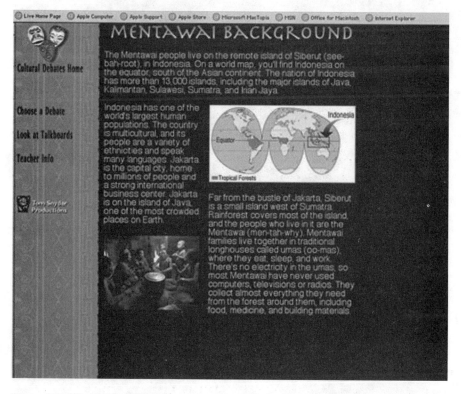

Figure 3.2. The *Cultural Debates* page containing background on the Metawi Tribe (Tom Snyder Productions, n.d.).

Tom Snyder Productions Web site suggests, learners can make their own cultural debate about their community for the Student Showcase.

While involved in content-based learning, these learners are also using oral language for a variety of purposes. The activity emphasizes the importance of linguistic skills, especially pronunciation because learners interact orally with their classmates and with learners across the Internet. Pragmatics also plays a role as learners work on discussion skills such as turn-taking and interrupting.

Example 3

▶ **Lesson:** Jazz Chants Online

Focus: Rhythm in oral English, adverbs of frequency, computer parts vocabulary, stress, pronunciation.

Preparation: Write a sentence on the board and review the terms *stress*, *intonation*, and *rhythm*. Discuss with students how these aspects in the target language may differ from these same aspects in their first language. Students can do some of the pronunciation exercises in *One Stop Magazine* (see Macmillan Publishers, 2004b) alone or in groups; then the class can practice with several sentences, marking the word stress and intonation patterns.

Presentation: Find "My computer's crashed" chant at the *One Stop English* site (Macmillan Publishers, 2004a). Print or copy the script for each student. Students listen to the recording on the Web site as they mark the stress and intonation patterns and take notes on any pronunciation aspects that they need. Students can listen as many times as they need to. They compare their marks with one or more classmate's and then the whole class corrects the marks on their scripts together.

Practice: Students practice the chant orally in groups or individually, and student listeners mark a script for student speakers to show the stress and intonation used. Speakers can then compare their performance to the corrected script.

Evaluation: Students can listen to, mark, and practice another chant from the Web site.

Extension: Learners pick a topic and find a partner. With their partner, learners then develop a jazz chant for the topic. They can record their chant for future class exercises, or they can present it to the class for evaluation and discussion.

Although this activity is focused on discrete skills, it provides learners with ample scaffolding and modeling, authentic audiences for their interaction, and many choices in their extension activity. In other words, this activity meets many of the conditions for language learning. As is evident from the examples in this chapter, computers can promote listening and speaking in many ways that meet the conditions for individual language learning.

▶ Conclusion

Many of the activities throughout this book support listening and speaking and meet conditions for language learning. These exercises and activities are only a small portion of those available for teachers and learners. For example, *One Stop Magazine* (see MacMillan Publishers, 2004c) has many great ideas for speaking activities in language classrooms. Although not presented as CALL activities, most of them (e.g., "The World's Funniest Joke") would be effective and enjoyable to do with online partners, especially using audio files sent through e-mail (i.e., audio e-mail). Beare (2003) provides technology-integrated lesson plans that show how such computer activities can complement in-class, face-to-face activities. At the *Sounds of English* Web site (Widmayer & Gray, 2002), learners can work on specific pronunciations with video support and do minimal pair work. For content-based listening, the movies at *BrainPOP* (http://www.brainpop.com/) are fabulous multimedia resources. Depending on your learners' and your goals, contexts, and needs, computer technologies are available to enhance skills and practice lessons of all kinds.

▶ Teachers' Voices

In years past, when I taught Language Arts, I would use music from School House Rock to enhance our lesson plans. For example, when we finished subject and predicates, we would learn and sing "Mr. Morton" ("Mr. Morton is the subject of my sentence. Whatever the predicate says he does. . . ."). They would learn some songs and perform in front of the class. I thought it was very effective because of the catchy way they learned the rules. Sometimes, I would have students come back as eighth graders to my class and resing those songs. It may sound corny, but it works!

Are you willing to take the risk of putting students on voice chat and audio e-mail? I have enough trouble getting the parents of my students to agree to let them use the Internet sources I have gathered—I know they would never allow me to arrange "chats" even for practice.

Earobics Step 1, for ages 4–7, and Earobics Step 2, for ages 7–10, produced by Cognitive Concepts, comes with inclusive user guides and resource manuals. Their audio, graphics, presentations, student evaluations (for student and teacher), entertaining characters, and games are fantastic. They focus on spoken sounds, contain programmed background noise in places, address sequential ordering, blend sounds, associate sound with letter or group of letters and much more. More information is at www.earobics.com.

When I first received my computers, I tried having large groups at a time go to the computer to teach specific skills. I found that it was not effective nor was it efficient, and that I was slowly going crazy. There were so many questions and problems; I became frustrated, as did my students. Then I changed the format of my computer time. I first showed the whole class what they would be learning on my projector. I then got my class started on independent work. Then I took a small group of seven back to the computers, taught them the skill we were currently working on and that they had just seen demonstrated, and got through the task. I then allowed each of those students to teach the skill to another student, who taught it to another student, and so on. It was a wonderful way for me to check the students' level of understanding on the computers, it gave the students an opportunity to show what they had learned in an authentic way, and it allowed me the opportunity to individually meet with students. It is a method that may not work for everybody; in my class it's great. I think it just showed me that in using technology within the classroom, each teacher needs to individualize the management aspect of it to suit their specific needs and comfort levels.

chapter 4

Communication and Collaboration

▶ **Focus**

In this chapter you will

- review the benefits of communication and collaboration in language classrooms

- learn techniques to support communication and collaboration

- discover opportunities afforded by a variety of physical contexts

- learn how technology can be used as communications medium to enhance classroom communication

- explore activities and tools that promote collaboration and communication

A s you read about the CALL project below, reflect on how students communicate and work together during the activity.

ESL students in Mr. Ehman's class in New York are involved in their Mystery Character assignment. They are conducting Internet and library research on a character that they have chosen from current political events. In each group, one student is assigned to research the character's background, one to discover information about the character's current situation, and one to uncover interesting little-known facts about the character. Group members will pool their information in order to pose as this famous mystery person. They compose an e-mail message in English to their native-English-speaking key pals (online pen pals) in Ohio with clues about their character's identity. Their pals will use clues from the messages, reference materials from their library, texts, classmates, and other resources to form questions to ask the mystery character. While trying to guess who the mystery character is, students are required to complete an individual written analysis of each message their group receives and then pool their answers with the group to decide what questions to ask. They also decide together what names to guess. After an exchange of several messages, the native speakers will eventually guess who the mystery person is. Once they guess correctly the roles will be reversed, with the native-English-speaking students sending the clues and the ESL students trying to guess the name of the new mystery character.

▶ Overview of Communication and Collaboration In CALL

As evidenced by the conditions and standards outlined in chapter 1, communication is a crucial component of language learning environments, including those enhanced by technology (Chapelle, 1998). Whereas the term *communication* implies simply conveying knowledge either one way or through an exchange, the term *collaboration* is less easy to define precisely. For the purposes of this book, collaboration will be taken to mean the process during which learners interact socially to create shared understandings (Nyikos & Hashimoto, 1997). Social interaction, one of the conditions defined in chapter 1, includes two or more participants communicating by negotiating meaning, clarifying for each other, and working in other ways to understand each other. Many educators believe that technology's capability to support communication and collaboration has changed the classroom more than any of its other capabilities. In fact, it is how educators make use of that capability that can change classroom goals, dynamics, turn-taking, interactions, audiences, atmosphere, and feedback and create a host of other learning opportunities.

The focus on social interaction as the basis for collaboration fits well with both the TESOL (1997) and NETS (ISTE, 2002b) standards; the NETS for students require student mastery of technology communication tools, including being able to "collaborate, publish, interact with peers, experts, and other audiences" and "use a variety of media and formats to communicate information and ideas effectively to multiple audiences" (Forcier & Descy, 2002, p. 421). By interacting and negotiating meaning with others in the target language, learners can

- take advantage of modeling
- gain new, comprehensible language input
- use language creatively
- work together to understand new experiences and derive meaning from them
- solve language and content problems
- gain control of a situation or person
- learn to use language appropriately
- transfer information
- focus on language structure and use (compiled from Warschauer, 1998)

Clearly, these benefits derive from interacting with other people who can respond creatively and originally in a focused way. Because computers available in classrooms cannot respond in such a way, computers cannot function as partners but instead function as tools during true collaboration. However, the effectiveness of the collaboration tool depends on many variables.

▶ Supporting Communication and Collaboration

Social interaction may take place in many configurations—for example, student to student, student to group, and group to group. Learners can also interact socially with a variety of people: classmates, teachers, students in other classes, community members, external experts, and peers around the world. In *CALL Environments* (Egbert & Hanson-Smith, 1999), Hanson-Smith and I described many ways to develop interactive technology-enhanced tasks for these different group arrangements and participants. We noted that because learners are put into work groups or asked to participate does not mean that they will interact, or that they will interact in the target language, or that the interaction will facilitate language learning. The teacher must plan carefully to ensure that the interaction is effective. Here are two techniques for helping teachers to develop tasks that increase the possibility of quality social interaction:

1. **Provide opportunities for learners to be active.**

   We have all been in study groups in which some students do the work and others do not participate. Those who do not participate may acquire some of the task's language or content, but they may also be missing out on the interaction they need to succeed. To help students become actively involved in the interaction, the teacher can build specific roles or assignments for individuals into tasks so that each student's contribution is necessary to achieve the group or team goal. These activity structures create the need for students to interact in the target language; the more learners need to interact, the more effective the interaction should be. These principles are the basis of techniques such as *cooperative learning* (Kagan, 1994; Richards & Lockhart, 1994), *jigsaw* (Peregoy & Boyle, 2001), and *information gap*.

2. **Provide reasons for learners to listen and respond.**

   Many times at the end of a group task, learners are required to present their products to the whole class. In reality, they are addressing their presentations to the teacher for evaluation. What reason do the other students have to attend to what is being presented? By providing reasons to listen, such as adding evaluation rubrics that the audience completes, providing a handout to take notes for a quiz, or requiring a group synthesis of the information presented, the teacher encourages all learners to listen and provides a basis from which to respond.

These techniques are related, in part, to the condition of autonomy (see chapter 1 for a discussion), in that the more choices (autonomy) the students have, the more they need to interact, consult, or negotiate with their team members and class.

In this chapter's opening scenario, Mr. Ehman has planned his task carefully to support student collaboration. First, the task requires his language students to interact with native speakers and with members of their teams in the target language. Second, students in Mr. Ehman's class have specific task roles. They must combine and synthesize the information they gather in their roles as researchers to develop a group message from their mystery character. This information gap activity, in which learners have information that their teammates do not, gives everyone in the group a reason to listen to the others' findings. In addition, by requiring students to analyze their incoming messages independently but using a handout to support group work, Mr. Ehman is also preparing his students to interact effectively. In the mystery character activity, the technology helps to create an environment unique in supporting interaction. In other activities the use of computers may play a more peripheral role.

Before discussing activities that support social interaction and collaboration in the CALL classroom, I want to briefly review the specific physical classroom contexts in which CALL occurs. Computers can be arranged in many different ways, ranging from complete labs to one-computer classrooms. The arrangement of the technology is one factor that impacts the potential for student interaction and collaboration, and teachers should consider the physical layout when designing CALL activities.

Interaction in the Computer Lab

In a traditional CALL lab layout, students are sequestered in their own carrels or are sitting behind the computers, which obstruct clear lines of sight to the rest of the room. Although labs seem to be falling out of fashion, they are useful not only for individual language learning activities such as using self-access software, conducting research, writing papers, sending e-mail, and completing practice exercises, but also for working on individual tasks as part of collaborations with online partners. However, the limited opportunities for mobility and difficulties in sharing hardware in a lab setting make collaborating face-to-face difficult for multiple learners; this setting is better used, then, for individual tasks or online collaboration.

Interaction in the Multiple-Computer Classroom

Computer classrooms, such as the one shown in Figure 4.1, allow for more group configurations and activities than traditional labs do. In this type of classroom, where computer monitors are recessed into desks and the desks arranged in pods of four or six, students have free lines of sight to each other and an unobstructed view of the teacher. Unlike the lab, the students have room to work without the computer and use it only when and if they need it. In this setting, the technology serves as a tool for all kinds of exercises, from building Web pages to creating portfolios to working with stand-alone software packages. Instructors in these settings can develop CALL tasks during which learners work with partners online and face-to-face. It is important to try out the furniture before buying it—not all desks are made the same, and buying the wrong furniture can be a pricey mistake.

Interaction in the One-Computer Classroom

U.S. public schools commonly provide each teacher with one computer, sometimes in addition to a shared lab facility in the school. Although one computer would seem to be insufficient for many CALL activities, the one-computer classroom has some benefits:

- The teacher can see what all learners are doing on the computer.
- The teacher has more control and more opportunities to directly facilitate interaction.
- The technology is available at any time.
- Students can see each other and work cooperatively without barriers.
- It is easier for the teacher to give feedback.
- Having only one computer shifts the focus from the technology to learning and interacting.
- It is easy to use a variety of group configurations.

Learners in one-computer settings typically do not collaborate with partners at a distance, but this is a rich context for face-to-face interaction. Much of the software and many of the activities described in this book are intended for use in the one-computer classroom.

Figure 4.1. A CALL classroom at Washington State University.

These three contexts—lab, multiple-computer classroom, and one-computer classroom—and other variations on technology-enhanced settings all support CALL activities. However, when designing CALL tasks, teachers must consider the physical setting's impact on not only the efficiency but also the effectiveness of language learning. In other words, for an activity that requires triads of learners to interact to be effective in a computer lab, it might also have to be adapted. Likewise, an activity presented as a teacher-fronted lesson might best occur in the regular, one-computer classroom.

▶ Tips for Designing a Computer-Enhanced Collaborative Project

In addition to making sure that students have opportunities to be active, reasons to listen and respond to each other, and an appropriate physical environment in which to work, teachers must consider other factors when designing effective computer-enhanced collaborative projects. First, teachers should consider what they know about their students and, as much as possible, tailor the conditions to students' needs and abilities. For example, if two students work better autonomously but others need more scaffolding and structure, their teachers should consider these needs when designing the project and choosing the tools. Second, developing effective groups will encourage effective interaction in the language classroom. Creating effective groups in technology-enhanced language learning classrooms requires the teacher to pay attention to the same factors as in any language learning situation, such as the students' first languages and cultures, educational backgrounds, and levels of target language proficiency. For group tasks that require students to use computers, the teacher may also need to consider students' levels of technical expertise and keyboarding proficiency. Third, it is important to make the technology fit the project and not vice versa. Although you may be tempted to design a project around software or a Web site that you really like, the project will more likely meet curriculum and other goals if you make those goals, and not the computer tool, the basis for the project. Fourth, consider what will encourage students to interact in the target language. If two or more students in the same group speak the same first language, make sure that they document their collaboration in English in some way. Finally, make sure that the outside experts, electronic mailing lists, or distant students with whom your students will interact have agreed to participate in the project and know what is expected of them. Following these tips will make your project more efficient and effective for all participants. Examples of how these tips work in practice are presented in the next section.

▶ Activities That Encourage Communication and Collaboration

As noted earlier, true social interaction cannot take place with the computer, but there are many ways it can occur through and around the technology. To show how the techniques for supporting communication and collaboration can be implemented, I describe CALL activities that provide opportunities for students to collaborate and communicate on some level. After each activity, I describe the computer tool, the students' roles, the choices they can make and need to discuss, and what encourages them to listen and respond to their peers or other information sources. The examples address learners in an assortment of grade and language levels from a variety of contexts and settings. I have divided them into stand-alone examples that use software on individual computers and online examples that use features of the Internet.

Activities Using Stand-Alone Software

The examples in this section focus on stand-alone, commercially developed software packages. Teachers can use the techniques and principles described previously to develop activities with many different types of software. One of the benefits of using stand-alone software packages is that they do not change, whereas Internet resources must be checked regularly for changes.

Putting Vocabulary Into Context

Diana and Evaristo are sitting together in the computer lab, but during this activity Diana is turned away from the computer screen. Evaristo is working on the "Your Environment" section of the lab's vocabulary software. As each word comes onto his screen, he dictates it aloud to Diana, who copies it onto her paper. They discuss which answer choice presents the meaning of the word and then Evaristo enters the answer into the software. If the answer is correct Diana writes the definition on the paper and they move on to the next word; if not, they discuss alternatives. When the exercise is finished correctly, Diana and Evaristo will study together for a vocabulary quiz.

Example 1

> **Tool:** vocabulary practice software
>
> **Interaction:** student pairs
>
> **Roles:** One student is the computer operator and the other the writer; during the next unit, they may switch roles.
>
> **Choices:** Students decide on their partners and roles.
>
> **Reason to listen and respond:** Students must cooperate to get all the words and definitions down on paper and to study for the quiz.

Learning About the United States

The National Inspirer (Version 1.0) simulation provides each student team with a set of six maps of the United States. Each map has information about a different aspect of the economy, geography, or demographics of each of the 50 states. The teacher sets the software for a specific number of teams, and the software gives each team a set of criteria that they must meet as they travel across 10 contiguous states. For example, a team may be given points for landing on states that are the largest producers of milk and states that have an average elevation of 200 feet, and they will be given extra points for ending up on a state that is one of the largest producers of copper. When any student team has its route prepared, it enters each state in the route into the computer and is given points at each state that meets the criteria. They are then given new criteria for the next trip.

Example 2

> **Tool:** National Inspirer (Version 1.0)
>
> **Interaction:** student and team members
>
> **Roles:** economist, demographer, population specialist, importer, geographer, and secretary
>
> **Choices:** Learners decide the manner in which their group will function (e.g., how they will get input from each other without looking at their maps). They also choose their route.

> **Reason to listen and respond:** Students will score the most points if they land in states that have more than one attribute, so they need to know what their teammates know. This is an information gap activity.

Neighborhood Trip

The class is preparing for a field trip around their community. While one group is developing a set of questions to answer and a second group is locating community members to talk to, a third group uses simple map-making software on the one computer in their classroom to make a community map. Each student in the map group has been assigned a particular component of the map to research and to add to the map. When the map is finished, the group presents it to the class, explaining the key that they developed together and how to use the map most effectively. The other groups share their questions and resources. After the field trip, the class collaborates to add interesting information and features to the map.

Example 3

> ▶ **Tool:** Neighborhood Map Machine (Version 2.0)
>
> **Interaction:** student and small group members, student and class
>
> **Roles:** researchers for houses, streets, buildings, signs, or landmarks (each does the part of the key related to his or her role)
>
> **Choices:** Students choose the roles they play and how to present their information.
>
> **Reason to listen and respond:** Students must use the map to find their way to various locations in the community.

Choices, Choices

Elementary school ESL students working with a software simulation have been presented with a problem: The soccer field at their school is dirty and not ready for the upcoming big game. Students have to solve the problem by choosing a goal and then making decisions along the way toward the goal.

The choices of goals are (a) make less trash, (b) have fun at recess, (c) keep the playing field clean, and (d) win the soccer game. Learners in teams play roles within their group as they discuss each of the four choices of action, make decisions, and defend their decisions. The teacher or a student uses the software to click on the students' choice, and participants receive feedback and another set of choices. At the end of the simulation, the software helps students review their decisions and the outcomes and see how close they came to their goal.

Example 4

> ► **Tool:** Choices, Choices: Kids and the Environment (Version 1.0)
>
> **Interaction:** student and team members, teacher, or class
>
> **Roles:** Students each support one of the four different goals and make decisions based on their goal.
>
> **Choices:** Students decide how their group functions; they discuss and make their choices.
>
> **Reason to listen and respond:** To meet the goal, students need to be able to make informed decisions.

Activities Using Online Resources

The Mystery Character activity in the introduction to this chapter is an example of a computer-enhanced task that supports many kinds of communication and collaboration between members of the group and between on-site and off-site groups. Other online activities that support interaction are developing advertisements, participating in a literature circle, and completing or developing WebQuests.

Shopping on the Web

Student teams are asked to develop a new advertising campaign for a common product. Before doing so, they need to compare their product's existing prices, features, and advertising. Each student checks a different Web site, such as http://www.amazon.com/, http://www.buynow.com/, or another shopping site that the teacher has supplied and then fills out a column in the product comparison handout. The other team members add the information that they have discovered about the product. They will use this information as they take on the roles of artist, text editor, and presentation specialist in preparing their advertising campaign. Once their advertising is in place, they will present it to the class for evaluation. Students will also take orders for the product from members of the school community as a way to evaluate their work.

Example 5

> **Tool:** Internet shopping sites and advertising, presentation/ graphics package such as Microsoft PowerPoint, word processor
>
> **Interaction:** student and small group members, small group and class, small group and school
>
> **Roles:** In the first part, students are all researchers at different sites for the product. In the second part, they each take a role in developing the advertising.
>
> **Choices:** They choose a product that they are interested in, choose Web sites to visit from the teacher's list, and develop their own advertising strategy and presentation format.
>
> **Reason to listen and respond:** The audience must evaluate whether the advertising is effective and tell why.

Reading Circles

Students are required to post a weekly reading reflection to their class's online conference on http://www.blackboard.com. They are working with students at two other schools who are reading the same articles as they are each week. To keep the discussion going, the teacher has assigned each student to reply also to two other students' reflections each week during lab time. Students can ask questions, clarify points about the readings, or persuade the other students to their point of view. At the end of the week, each student writes a summary in his or her reading journal of what he or she learned from the week's online discussion and then takes a quiz on the reading content.

Example 6

> ► **Tool:** asynchronous electronic discussion forum
>
> **Interaction:** student and off-site partners, student and whole group, student and teacher
>
> **Roles:** Each student posts an individual opinion.
>
> **Choices:** Students choose what to say and to whom they say it.
>
> **Reason to listen and respond:** Students must understand the issues to participate in the discussion, and they have to pass the quiz.

WebQuests

In Ms. Hall's class, high school ESL students are working on the "Are you what you eat?" WebQuest that she developed. Their task is to create a cookbook of healthy regional recipes from the United States. Each team is assigned to one region of the United States and is required to

- make a list of foods specific to the region and investigate their history
- design a sample menu of ethnic foods for their region from that list, including entree, starch, vegetable, bread, dessert, and beverage. Including salad gets extra points.
- obtain sample recipes for these foods by searching the Internet or by conferencing over the Internet with a chef
- analyze each recipe on the menu for nutrients and construct a table for each recipe with the nutrient analysis
- total the nutrients for each complete menu and determine whether or not the menu is healthy using the American Heart Association's Dietary Guidelines for Healthy American Adults. If the menu is not healthy, use the guidelines for lowering fat and cholesterol to revise the recipes.
- prepare all healthy recipes for the class to sample, and submit them in recipe format to be placed in the cookbook (Hall, 2001)

The students divide up the research tasks among themselves to use their time efficiently. They use the roles that Ms. Hall recommends: (a) historian to research how the history and development or settlement of each region influenced the region's foods; (b) journalist to record the information found during the learning process and to lay out the menu and recipes for placement in the cookbook; and (c) food researcher or nutritionist to interpret and analyze the foods, recipes, and other nutritional information discovered during the quest. The students compile all of their information to develop their final menu and prepare their meal.

Example 7

> ▶ **Tool:** WebQuest, Internet sites, word processor
>
> **Interaction:** student and small group members, small group to class, student or small group to external experts (chefs, for example)
>
> **Roles:** Each student contributes part of the information needed to complete the project.
>
> **Choices:** Students choose their roles, where and how they find their information, and how to present it.
>
> **Reason to listen and respond:** The audience must listen to know what they are eating and why and to provide feedback.

These examples demonstrate that many different activities can support communication and collaboration in language classrooms. There are also many tools to facilitate such interaction.

▶ Tools for Communication and Collaboration

In addition to the tools just mentioned, those described in this section have been used in a variety of ways in CALL classrooms. Communication and collaboration using software and Internet tools can happen synchronously (at the same time) or asynchronously (learners posting at different times), and, depending on the goal, both can be useful in language classrooms.

MOO

A MOO (multi-user object-oriented domain) is a text-based program that runs on a computer and can be accessed by a large number of users from all over the world at the same time. Typically MOOs provide a map of locations and a help screen to show users how to get around. In this electronic environment, users can type in words to chat with other users synchronously and commands to explore other aspects of the virtual world. MOOs are useful for learning map skills, working in text, and interacting with other users worldwide. Some MOOs have themes; examples include *schMOOze* (http://schmooze.hunter.cuny.edu/), *LinguaMOO* (http://lingua.utdallas.edu/), *Tapped In* (http://www.tappedin.org/), *Active Worlds* (http://activeworlds .com), and *Zing* (http://www.zing.com).

Chat

A chat room is a Web site that provides a forum for users to communicate in real time (synchronously). It is used for interactive messaging. Special software is not usually needed. Chatting is especially useful for interviews, guest lectures, and discussions in which instructors want everyone to have a chance to participate. Sometimes the conversation scrolls very quickly out of sight, however, and messages are not always in order. Examples include *MSN Messenger* (http://messenger.msn.com/), *Yahoo Messenger* (http://messenger .yahoo.com/), and *ICQ* (http://web.icq.com/).

Discussion Forums

Forums provide asynchronous written conversation. Benefits include allowing students more time to think before they post and posting in themed threads that may be easier to read and follow than chats. Examples include electronic discussion forums often found in commercial courseware packages such as Blackboard (available from http://www.blackboard.com/), WebWorkZone (available from http://webworkzone.com/), and the Daedalus Integrated Writing Environment (available from http://www.daedalus.com/). Some are also free, such as Yahoo groups (http://groups.yahoo.com/). Figure 4.2 presents the interface of the Virtual Teacher Community electronic discussion forum.

Electronic Lists

Electronic lists, sometimes called *listservs* after a piece of popular proprietary software used to set up and run the list, are e-mail posting services created to facilitate the exchange of information. When an e-mail message is sent to a mailing list, it is automatically broadcast to everyone who is subscribed to the list. An example is LaTrobe University's *Student Project List* (http://sl-lists.net/).

Software

Although the Internet is the most obvious source for collaboration tools, software packages can also support collaboration and communication. In addition to the software packages already mentioned, common software

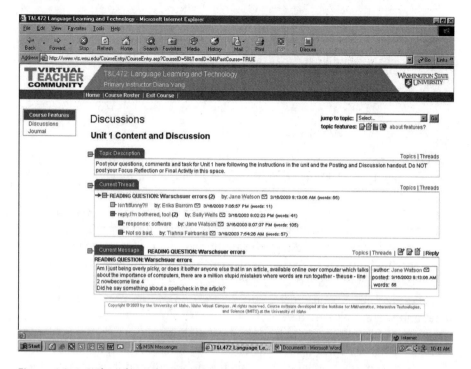

Figure 4.2. Interface from the Virtual Teacher Community electronic forum.

packages such as word processing programs can be used for collaboration. For example, the "comment" function in Microsoft Word allows learners to work together and comment on each other's work.

These tools support opportunities for English language learners to work with others for a wide variety of tasks and collaborations. These technologies can clearly help classroom environments to meet the conditions for optimal learning. More important than how they connect learners, however, is why and with whom learners connect.

▶ Conclusion

This chapter has presented some of the ways that language learners can interact socially and shown how both teachers and learners can use technology to support and encourage collaboration. Each of the activities provides students with specific roles to play that are important to the outcome of the task, gives them choices so that they must discuss and plan, and provides them with important reasons to listen and respond to each other. Even these task features do not guarantee that learners will interact and learn, but chances are better that they will than if the tasks are not planned to enhance interaction.

▶ Teachers' Voices

I would like to share a project that our Technology Coordinator shared with us yesterday. I am planning to do it with my bilingual students and another classroom next school year. It is called "The Monster Exchange," and it is designed to encourage the development of reading and writing skills while integrating Internet technology into the classroom curriculum. You can find more about this project at this Web site: http://www.monsterexchange.org/. Last year, the high school ESL students participated in this activity together with students learning Spanish. The identity of the partners that are . . . working together remains anonymous till the end of the task. Then they meet and share their experience.

As far as other activities that might be helpful, I think you can also have the students record what they want to say in KidPix and send it as an e-card to each other (since your focus at this point seems more communication and getting them motivated), or they can even record what they want to say to an author and send it by e-mail.

These are the roles I use in my classroom—of course there are others and some worded differently, but these roles work well for my fifth graders: Manager, Timekeeper, Cheerleader, Taskmaster, Reporter.

Different titles are used depending on the activity: geographer, cartographer, text media, and so on. Most titles revolve around: recorder, presenter, timekeeper, organizer, facilitator. I give these roles names that are appropriate to the task.

First and foremost, just because students are in high school, it does not mean they are prepared to work with the latitude of issues associated with open forum discussion on the Internet; this is scary. Therefore boundaries must exist with regards to technology in K–12. I would not, however, rule out using e-mail in a structured, purposeful lesson. In terms of building language, MSN Chat is a great way for students to build their automaticity. I have found when students are really engaged that they amazingly come up with vocabulary and words that they themselves were not aware they knew.

The second reason I would structure and use e-mail and MS-type chatting in elementary school is to narrow the socioeconomic gap; other students have access to this in their homes and it provides rich experience that students may need later on down the road.

From Catherine Brown's resource handbook I found some information on how to start e-mail discussion groups. I didn't try any of this but it may be useful for some of you. E-mail discussion groups (students can post messages and receive messages posted to them from the subscribers).
To get started:

EslList macjord@oxnar-dsd.org (ages 11–16)
Dave's ESL Café http://www.eslcafe.com/

She also includes a list of Internet Web pages to obtain Key pals (inter-class, and inter-district, -region, -state, or -national):

Clases Gemelas from Nuava Alejandria http://www.nalejandria.com
E-Pals Classroom Exchange http://www.epals.com/

chapter 5

Creativity and Production

▶ Focus

In this chapter you will

- reflect on the benefits of language production for language fluency and accuracy

- learn techniques and guidelines for supporting student creativity and production

- explore activities and tasks that support student creativity and production

As you read the anecdote below, try to figure out all the ways that students can receive language input and produce language during the project.

High beginning-level English language learners in Mr. Lin's class are developing television and print ads for new products that they designed during a unit on advertising. Each team of three students has created and scanned a drawing of their product, and they have also developed a life-sized model for possible use in their TV commercial. Most of the students are now writing their ads. Mr. Lin watches as some of them are looking at commercials on the Internet to get ideas; other students seem to be debating the wording of their ads. By assigning each group member a role, Mr. Lin has made sure that each student is responsible for an important piece of the project. Because he also has a rule that students must ask three other students a question before they bring it to him, he sees a lot of intergroup interaction. When the students have completed the scripts for the TV and print versions of their ads, they will try them out on another group, who will suggest changes and other ideas before they go into production. Students will use the ESL program's new digital camera to film their TV ad and then edit it with iMovie (Version 3.0.3). They will create their print ad using FrontPage, Microsoft's Web page editor software. Final versions of both ads will be posted to the Web, along with an explanation of the assignment and a reflection on the different processes and ideas behind the two types of ads. Students will then have the opportunity to obtain feedback from their classmates and from outside experts.

▶ Overview of Creativity and Production in Language Learning

Creativity and production are related to many of the conditions for optimal language learning. Although most researchers agree that *input* is important for language learning (see, e.g., Long, 1989, 1996; Pica 1994), they have only recently begun to explore the important role of *output*, or language production, in language acquisition (Holliday, 1999; Swain, 1995). Production is important because it allows students to test their hypotheses about how language works and encourages students to use their preferred learning styles to gain additional input in the target language.

Social interaction not only enables valuable language input, but it also enables valuable language production. It allows learners to understand when others find their language incomprehensible and gives them an opportunity to explore various ways of making themselves understood. Feedback from others can also help them notice the discrete grammatical items that they need to focus on to improve their language. Language and content output can take many forms (e.g., speech, graphics, text), and it can range from essays to multimedia presentations.

Producing language assists the language learning process in many ways, but production does not in and of itself promote learning. For example, production can include relatively meaningless activities such as reciting answers to uncontextualized grammar drills. Creativity implies something more—doing something original, adapting, or changing. In this sense, a sentence or a presentation in language classrooms can be creative. To be creative, students need opportunities for intentional cognition; appropriate support, scaffolding, and feedback; and control over language aspects that they will use in their production. Working with others (see chapter 4) often facilitates creativity.

These two goals—production and creativity—are often tied together in the literature. For example, the third goal of the *National Educational Technology Foundation Standards for Students* (ISTE, 2002b) requires that "students use technology tools to enhance learning, increase productivity, and promote creativity" (Forcier & Descy, 2002, p. 381). The TESOL standards suggest that language should be used in the same way. *Productivity tools* maximize or extend students' ability to create products and to problem-solve; they also "expand opportunities for expression" (Male, 1997, p. viii), which is an important principle for language learning. Productivity and creativity tools support students in constructing models, publishing, planning and organizing, mapping concepts, generating material, collecting data, and developing and presenting other creative works. Even in productions that do not use language per se, learners work through the language to produce.

Examples of commonly used productivity tools include word processors, databases, spreadsheets, desktop publishers, graphics programs, hypertext mark-up language (html) editors, and, in some instances, e-mail and other communications technologies. These technologies enable English language learners to choose their own content and provide templates and functions that scaffold their presentation of content. These tools do not make learners more creative or their products better, but some research shows that these tools encourage learners to produce more and to use their creativity. The more creative output students produce, the more opportunities they have to learn.

Productivity tools also provide opportunities for teachers. All of the technologies mentioned, along with grading programs, worksheet- and puzzle-making software, and presentation packages, help teachers to create products to use in their classes and to improve their instructional processes (for more on teacher tools, see chapter 10). Teacher and student products and the results of their creative processes abound on the World Wide Web. A review of some of the Web sites that contain such examples can inspire teachers and learners to integrate and use production and creativity tools in their teaching and learning. It must be noted, however, that merely using these tools does not result in language learning. Teachers must carefully plan and adapt activities and tasks so that they meet language learning goals.

▶ Supporting Creativity and Production

Below are two instructional techniques that support the conditions for language learning and facilitate student creativity and production.

1. **Do not do what students can do.**
   Teachers must give students choices and support their autonomy by allowing them to learn by doing. In many classrooms, however, teachers take full responsibility for planning lessons, developing materials, directing activities, and assessing students. Allowing students to help with the design and delivery of instruction gives them more opportunities to interact, to problem-solve (discussed in chapter 6) and use language creatively.

2. **Let learners show what they can do, rather than what they cannot.**
   This era of high-stakes testing mandates that teachers know what their students cannot do. They often assess students on very discrete language items using multiple choice, true/false, or fill-in-the-blank answers. Although these tests can provide certain kinds of information, allowing students to produce language or content in a variety of ways that support their interlanguage (their individual language system) builds on student successes and helps students to understand that they can communicate in different modes. At the same time, this practice demonstrates to students that they have control over content and language.

In this chapter's opening scenario, Mr. Lin's language learners have the opportunity to produce language both orally and in written form, and they produce language and creative content for many reasons. They make decisions, ask questions, write dialogue, draw, role-play, direct, suggest, critique, and disagree. Students who are not as competent in one area may choose to produce language in other areas, but none of the students is exempt from working toward the final goal. By requiring that learners ask each other for help, Mr. Lin is not doing what he knows that his learners can do; rather, he is providing frameworks of support.

▶ Tips for Designing Opportunities for Creativity And Production

There are several other important ways to design activities that support student creativity and production and therefore afford opportunities for language learning. First, students must understand how to use the computer tools. This information should be presented in a variety of ways—graphically, orally, and in text at a minimum. Students must also understand the opportunities that the tool affords. To this end, teachers and learners can brainstorm the kinds of tasks that can be accomplished with tools such as a database program, a word processor, or a graphic organizer, and they can continue to add to the list over time so that students are not limited in the ways in which they produce content and language. While learning the technologies, students are also learning through English, both useful goals in the CALL classroom.

▶ Activities That Encourage Creativity and Production

Many of the activities presented throughout this book also support creativity and production, especially the WebQuests. These activities also meet other conditions for language learning, including social interaction, authentic tasks, and learner autonomy.

In developing tasks and activities that encourage creativity and production, teachers and students should reflect on why to use technology. As discussed earlier, if the technology does not make the process or product more effective or more efficient, teachers and learners should consider other tools. For example, many English language learners are asked to produce a text-based Web page to introduce themselves to others. Because Web pages often use relatively few media, it might be more useful, depending on the teachers' goals, to have students develop richer products such as video footage, an electronic photo montage, or a short multimedia book. However, learners may get caught up in the graphics and lose opportunities for language learning—teachers must make sure that the task is devised so that learners focus on using language. In another project, where secondary school English language learners create multimedia books for elementary school English language learners, the multimedia features can make the text more accessible, provide many types of input and opportunities for output, and make an elementary school audience more likely to respond to the content. By focusing on the importance of text, teachers can help learners use the technology's features to provide the young learners with a whole literacy experience.

Helping language learners to create and produce effectively might seem like an overwhelming task at this point; however, by focusing on the principled use of technology, the number of possible tasks is almost limitless. Although I have tried to avoid focusing on the technology over the task and goals (in other words, I try not to fall into technocentrism), I have divided the examples below into three categories to demonstrate that creativity and production result not from the technology used, but from the task structure. The example task categories are (a) those that require basic technologies, (b) those that call for the use of relatively more sophisticated technologies, and (c) those that require the use of advanced technologies.

The examples below do not include the whole lesson plan and are not addressed to specific grade or language levels, although some possible language objectives are listed for each activity. All of them can be adapted to use different technologies and to work in different contexts.

Creativity and Production With Basic Technologies

Create a Wanted Poster

This activity will help students to understand U.S. culture, and to practice present tense and forming sentences. Students complete the following steps:

- find a photo of a person (magazine, Web, or personal). The teacher can choose a theme if desired (movie stars, historical figures, etc.).
- develop text about that person that fits the format of a wanted poster

He is a famous author. He is dead now. He wrote some books about adventures. Some of his books are banned. He was born in November. A.K.A. Samuel Clemens.

Mark Twain Visual by www.PDImages.com

Figure 5.1. Example of a wanted poster.

- type the text using appropriate fonts and styles, leaving room for the photo
- affix or insert the photo and post

Students get very creative with this activity, especially when they use photos of movie stars, international leaders, and white-collar criminals. (*Time* magazine is a great place for photos; see http://www.time.com/.) Follow up by covering the photos and having learners guess who the wanted character is from the text.

Produce a Résumé

This activity will help learners to practice listening for discrete information, organizing writing, forming questions, and using past tense. Instead of typing their own résumés, learners

- develop an interview scheme based on information required for résumés
- interview a classmate
- create their classmate's résumé using a word processor
- read and suggest revisions to their own résumé
- revise the résumé they typed
- present their classmate to the class

This activity facilitates extensive interaction among students and helps students to understand elements of résumés.

Create Holiday Cards

This activity will enable students to practice with culture, slang, and audience. They invent their own holidays, and then

- develop symbols for that holiday
- decide on the holiday's slogan
- create a holiday card(s) addressed to a specific audience(s) using a word processor and any available graphics. If available, they can be printed on greeting card stock.
- develop a plan for marketing their holiday and cards

During this activity students learn about cultural (and political) traditions while addressing their own interests. Happy Peanut Butter Day, everyone!

Develop a Simple Newsletter

This activity, which is common in both ESL and EFL classes, enables students to practice forming questions, scanning, reporting, and using adverbs of time. Students complete the following steps:

- collect information through interviews, literature reviews, and other means
- type their articles using a word processor
- take any photographs necessary or available
- work with classmates to edit, headline, and lay out the articles
- copy and deliver the newsletter to relevant parties

Some of the most interesting newsletters are often the simplest ones.

Generate T-Shirts and Bumper Stickers

This activity will enable students to practice idioms, slang, and humor. Students can accomplish it in many ways, but in general, they

- develop slogans or sayings based on their study of idiomatic English, the purpose for displaying slogans, and their own personal experiences
- revise based on classmates' or others' comments
- type their sayings into a word processor
- print with special bumper sticker or t-shirt iron-on paper
- display

Even students at beginning proficiency levels can come up with some witty and thoughtful sayings for this activity, and it can be integrated easily into content-area study.

Creativity and Production With More Sophisticated Technologies

Books for Younger or Less Proficient Students

The activity enables students to practice narrative, discussion, and reading aloud. Students complete the following activities:

- develop stories in cooperative groups in a chosen genre
- use HyperStudio (Version 3.0) or Microsoft PowerPoint to develop multimedia texts
- illustrate and edit with peers
- share with the intended audience

Addressing an authentic audience that differs from one's peers requires students to think about how to do it. At the same time, learners realize more about different language levels and how to work with others at these levels. One enjoyable tool to incorporate into this activity is Vox Proxy (Version 2.0). Once installed, this software program runs directly in PowerPoint and enables learners to program animated characters to participate in their presentations through narration and action. Because the software can recognize five languages, learners can even develop projects in their younger partners' native languages. Figure 5.2 shows "Janet" on the first page of a multimedia PowerPoint book, ready to explain the book to the reader.

Action Mazes

In this activity, students can practice connectors, story writing, and discussion. In collaborative groups, students

- decide on a topic and layout for their maze
- write the text and decide how it will branch at decision points
- find or create necessary graphics

Figure 5.2. "Janet" from VoxProxy in a multimedia PowerPoint book.

- create the maze in an authoring program such as HyperStudio (Version 3.0), Microsoft PowerPoint, or Quandary (Version 2.1), which is software specifically made to author action mazes
- share it with peers

Action mazes (Egbert, 1995; Healey, 2002; Holmes, 2002) facilitate discussion, collaboration, and creativity in both the creators and the users.

Ideal Neighborhood Map

This activity enables learners to practice present tense, local vocabulary, and culture. In teams, they

- brainstorm features of their neighborhood that they like
- reflect on what is missing and what else they would like to see
- agree on what their ideal neighborhood would look like
- use a program such as Inspiration (Version 6.0) or Neighborhood Map Machine (Version 2.0) to create the map
- present to peers, trying to get votes as ideal or most nearly ideal

This activity can lead to many others in which learners talk about their situations, and it could be the precursor to a community service learning activity.

Us Presentations

Learners practice comparatives, descriptive vocabulary, and presentation skills. In heterogeneous, cross-level, and cross-age groups, learners

- brainstorm similarities and differences among themselves
- choose a focus for their slide show
- design their show on paper, each learner creating at least one slide
- create the multimedia slide show using Kid Pix (Version 3.0) or Microsoft PowerPoint
- present the show and answer questions

By creating and producing with others, learners improve their language abilities while also increasing their cultural capital.

Interactive Quizzes

This activity enables learners to practice forming questions and statements, and explaining. Working alone or in groups, they

- choose format, questions, and answers for their quiz (also feedback)
- create their quiz in Hot Potatoes (Version 6.0), HyperStudio (Version 3.0), or another authoring/authorable program
- give their quiz and take other students' quizzes to help them study for the teacher's version

This activity is a good example of letting students show what they know. It also reinforces right answers and helps learners to understand plausible mistakes.

Creativity and Production With Advanced Technologies

New World Catalog

Learners practice future tense, conditionals, and descriptive language. Working together, they

- design products for the world that they would like to live in (e.g., if they choose a less polluted world as their goal, they might design clean cars, baby diapers that disintegrate upon removal, and sun-powered refrigerators)
- write text and add graphics to advertise each product
- put the catalog together using an advanced desktop publishing program
- print in color and share or post

This activity can also be done more simply using a word processor. During this activity, students need to reflect, predict, and create using the target language.

Digital Montages of Life in the United States

In this activity, students practice spoken narrative and fluency, and they learn about U.S. culture. To complete it, they

- plan and organize by creating a storyboard using Inspiration (Version 6.0) or another brainstorming and planning tool
- take photos of their subject using digital cameras (still or video)
- record the voiceover
- compile their movie with video creation software, such as iMovie (Version 3.0.3) or Avid Cinema (Version 1.0)
- post to the Web, present to peers, trade with other schools

These technologies seem advanced but only because they are expensive. They are easy to use even for elementary school learners. The Web has many examples.

Coauthor a Story Using Electronic Conferencing Software

This project enables learners to practice turn-taking and other pragmatics, narrative or storytelling, and editing. Working with learners at a remote site, they use desktop video conferencing or text conferencing to

- collaborate to decide on a topic and a plan
- assign roles
- write and edit the story
- post it to an agreed-upon site for further comment from other groups

This kind of activity requires the learners and the teacher to persevere and be patient, but the results can be worth it, and the social interaction definitely is.

Assemble Electronic Portfolios and Burn Them to CDs

In this activity, students practice reflection and presentation of language, and teachers have an opportunity to assess student learning. Teachers and students

- agree at the beginning of the term on the portfolio contents and format
- save portfolio components in electronic formats
- organize the components and burn them to CD or DVD

Students can take responsibility for their own learning in language, content, and technology skills.

Interactive Web Pages

Creating Web pages enables students to practice technical vocabulary and grammar for publication, and they have to think about audience. They can create all kinds of activities as they

- create a storyboard for their Web page or site
- gather tools
- use Flash (Version 5.0), Dreamweaver (Version 4.0), Director (Version 8.5), and other advanced technologies to make their pages interactive
- post their pages for other language learners to use or comment on

If teachers have a good reason to do it, teaching learners through and about advanced technologies can help them accomplish many language and content goals while also teaching them valuable technology skills.

These examples are only a few activities that facilitate language production and creativity. This book contains many others and the Web has even more examples. Teachers who want to design CALL activities that promote creativity and production should keep in mind the framework for language learning presented in chapter 1 and reflect on opportunities that the activities offer students to create and produce.

▶ Tools for Creativity and Production

The tools noted in the examples described earlier are *content-free;* in other words, they do not have any preset substance. With a little creativity, however, the teacher can use almost any computer tool to facilitate production and creativity. Even grammar drill and practice software can support creativity and production if used in a principled way. Here is an example of one way to do that (adapted from Egbert, Yang, & Hogan, 2003):

Two students are working on a 10-question grammar drill about past-tense verb forms. The program presents each fill-in-the-blank question separately, uncontextualized from the rest of the sentences in the drill. Student A works at the computer; Student B sits close but cannot see the screen.

- Student A reads each question presented on the screen while Student B writes the question down on a piece of paper, writing odd numbered questions on the left side of the paper, even numbered on the right.
- Student A reads the four possible answers (or reads the first answer, and if the students think it is wrong, goes to the next, and so on). The students choose the answer together, Student A checks it with the software, and Student B writes down the correct one and repeats the completed sentence out loud.
- The paper is divided between the columns. Student A takes one set of sentences and Student B takes the other. Now Student B sits at the computer, while Student A sits close by.
- The students interact, not showing each other their sentences, and try to put them together into a cohesive story. They can use dictionaries and any other resources they need. Student B types the story as they agree on it, and reads it aloud for Student A's approval.
- They share their stories with other groups who used the same sentences for their stories.

This activity works with adaptations even with large groups of students in one-computer classrooms. In such a case, while the teacher or other person reads the sentences, students can take the role of A or B to write down odd or even numbered sentences. They then pair up to write the story. During this activity both students have had multiple and multimodal exposure to all of the sentences, and both have produced each one more than once. Because their sentences have different contexts, they must be very creative to pull them all together into a story that makes sense.

▶ Conclusion

This chapter discussed the importance of production and creativity in language learning and presented examples of ways that computers can assist learners to produce and create. Production of this kind takes time, but it is time well spent when even learners with beginning proficiency in the target language are involved in thinking creatively about language and content and also working on the language skills that make their products presentable to an authentic audience.

▶ Teachers' Voices

Visual Communicator (by Serious Magic, http://www.seriousmagic.com/) allows students to make up video presentations. I don't have it, but I have seen it demonstrated. The kit costs about $150. It comes with the software, green fabric for background, and a clip-on microphone. The students prepare their presentation, enter it into the computer, and the software turns the computer into a teleprompter. A video camera is needed. It records the student at the computer reading from the teleprompter, but it looks like they are looking straight at the camera. That video is then tweaked through the computer. Since the kids are in front of the green background, they can add just about any new background through the editing process. It can look like they are at the beach in front of any famous landmark, or on the moon. The software comes with lots of backgrounds, and I think you can add your own, too. Then the students can polish it up. They can add a picture in a picture effect, so it looks like two people are talking to one another from different locations. They can make it look like the student is sitting at a nice desk in a newsroom setting, it can even add shadows. Of course music can be added, too. What really impressed me was how easy it looked to do all of this. The possibilities for this type of software seem huge. It can be used not only for newscast presentations, but for informative science lessons, for book review, electronic portfolios—parent conferences.

Filamentality is a program that helps educators learn how to create their own websites. http://www.kn.pacbell.com/wired/fil

The only thing I want to add about making a WebQuest is the server space. Yahoo and Geocities provide free server space. If you want to put your WebQuest online, those two can be your option, too.

We did an "All about me" activity where the students created a presentation about themselves. My global languages class created presentations on Jamaica when we researched the country. A third activity that my students have done was create an informative presentation on volcanoes. The students enjoy this because they are able to create colorful backgrounds, interesting transitions, sounds, and animations with their project.

I was using some of my software with my students for reviewing concepts, with not much way to check the effectiveness of it. Something that I discovered and that I always dreaded to get too much into it, since I have a million other things to do, is the binders that come with school edition software. I used it before for exploring different activities that can be done with Kid Pix. They all suggest ideas to expand the use of software. It also contains technical tips for teachers, thematic unit activities and additional bibliography. They can be adapted to the particular needs of my students and learning goals. Sometimes it gives you tips in how to import some of the graphics to another program to use them as one more resource to create an external document.

I ran across a site that recommends sites for your students to evaluate. One of them was the AFDB or the "Aluminum Foil Deflector Beanie, An effective, Low-Cost Solution to Combating Mind Control." Great site! Anyway, after discussing it with my principal, I managed to "con" another teacher into going along with my plans and during my 7/8th Leadership class and her 7th Language Arts class, we told the students that we were going to play a joke on the principal and all wear Aluminum Foil Deflector Beanies to lunch. My students really got into the game and created outstanding aluminum beanies, and as a group we went to lunch to surprise the principal. One of the students told me it was the "funnest" class ever, not knowing that the prank was really on them. The principal requested that I do it again next year as part of my curriculum! I have found so many things to do with my students, it's hard to pick!

My wife is a dancer and a person who values the creative process. She has vast experience in unlocking people's creative potential. She has a quote, from an unknown source in her office: Creativity is the balance between the expected and the unexpected. I agree with the two techniques addressed in this chapter, but I would like to add a third. We forget that it is difficult to be creative without some mastery within the field. Our creative geniuses have all been leaders within their field. It was from their mastery that they were able to go beyond mere correctness and into the realm of the unexpected and unknown. So I propose a third instructional technique to support creativity, a focus on mastery.

It is really hard to get a classroom full of elementary kids to complete some of these activities with some of the productivity software. In the past, I have really had a hard time with that and felt I just couldn't take the time from the school day to do it. I got a grant about 4 years ago to purchase little battery-powered word processors for each student. They are called AlphaSmarts. With those, everybody does their 1st draft on the AlphaSmart and then the revisions are really quick. After editing, they then go to the computer for formatting. It works really well.

chapter 6

> ## Inquiry and Problem-Solving

> ## Focus

In this chapter you will

- reflect on the kinds of skills students need to develop and use in language learning and the roles that inquiry and problem-solving play in this development

- learn about frameworks and technologies that can support inquiry and problem-solving

- reflect on content and language needs that can be met through computer-enhanced inquiry and problem-solving

$\mathbf{A}$s you read the scenario below, reflect on how problem-solving and language learning complement each other.

Ms. Petrie's sixth-grade ESL class has voiced a desire to learn more about U.S. culture. Throughout the first part of the semester the students made a list of questions that they would like to ask long-time residents of the United States. Ms. Petrie is working with the students to develop ways to answer their inquiries. She is basing the project on the outline provided by the Cultural Reporter (Version 1.0) materials that her school owns. First, she will show some of the video segments to help students reflect on what they really want to know. Second, she will work on techniques in the workbook to help them develop ways to find out information. Each student team will make a project plan in which they will outline their goals, list their questions, and describe how they will conduct their research, what resources they will use, and how they plan to present the results. The class decides that they will have a miniconference where they will present and discuss their results.

Team 1 has decided to interview native English speakers to learn their views about English language learners. They will produce a photo narrative of their experiences. Team 2 has decided to make a short video on what it is like to be a seventh grader. Other teams will approach community members to learn more about U.S. customs and beliefs. Each student will have a role. Students will keep a journal in which they record language, content, and process questions for discussion. In this way, they will receive helpful feedback and support during the project from peers and the teacher.

▶ Overview of Inquiry and Problem-Solving

Inquiry, for the purposes of this chapter, is defined as a process of discovery in which students go through iterative stages of questioning, reflecting, and research. Students can participate in many types of inquiry activities, including, for example, library research on historical events, constructing family genealogies, examining how their community supports environmental health, and exploring how different cultures are treated in their school. *Problem-solving* is often viewed as a component of these inquiry activities. Although difficult to define precisely, problem-solving is generally understood to include skills such as making accurate observations, finding and organizing information, predicting, synthesizing, and using other higher order thinking skills to find solutions.

Inquiry and problem-solving have been proposed as necessary for language learning for many years (Brown, 1994). Standards in many education fields, including the national ESL standards (see chapter 1; also TESOL, 1997, standards for Goal 2) and the NETS (ISTE, 2000, see Standards 5 and 6), also list inquiry and problem-solving as necessary skills.

Why do language students need to problem-solve and conduct inquiry? First, problem-solving and inquiry help students learn metacognitive strategies, and students who can use these strategies are typically better language learners. In addition, research indicates that learners remember better what they do rather than what they receive passively, and inquiry and problem-solving are active processes. As learners work to construct the language that they need while participating in problem-solving and inquiry tasks, they acquire additional languages in much the same way as they acquire their first—by trial and error, reflection, and personal involvement.

Second, in lessons where language is the content, students can apply strategies based on problem-solving and inquiry to recognize patterns, ask important questions, and make conclusions about language. The research is unclear, however, about whether these skills should be acquired from participating in problem-solving activities or if they should be taught before problems are presented.

Computer technologies can enhance language and content learning during inquiry and problem-solving activities in English language classrooms. First, computer technologies can support inquiry. For example, Encarta (n.v.) software provides a CD-based encyclopedia presented in multimedia format so that learners can see, listen to, read, and interact with the information that they are seeking. This format makes the language and content accessible for use in the problem-solving process. Another example is database or spreadsheet software that enables students to log and locate the data that they have collected during their inquiry. This software allows students to have a record of their process and the language involved in it. In addition, computer technologies can help students present the results of their inquiry projects (see chapter 5).

Problem-solving tools abound on the Internet, for example, *Filling the Toolbox* (McKenzie & Bryce Davis, 1986) and the *NASA SciFiles Instructional Tools* (Pinelli, 2004). Figure 6.1 presents some of the tools available through the *NASA SciFiles*.

Software publishers such as Tom Snyder Productions (http://www .tomsnyder.com/) offer a variety of software appropriate for various grades, types of content, and diverse learners that provides scaffolding to solve

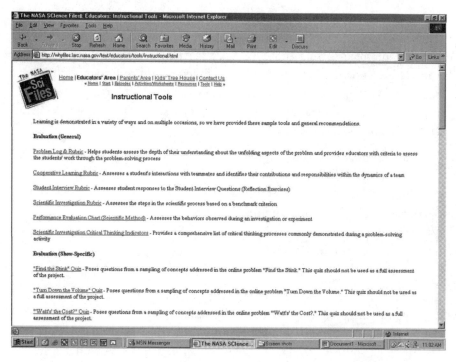

Figure 6.1. Some of the useful inquiry and problem-solving tools available from the *NASA SciFiles.*

problems in areas such as the environment, social relations, and immigration. Content-free graphical software such as Inspiration (Version 6.0) can help students use language to plan and organize during the inquiry and problem-solving process. In other words, computer-based resources can provide data on a wide range of topics that is accessible to students at different levels and with different learning styles and strategies, support the efficient organization of data, facilitate an organized and accessible presentation, and present problems, all while tracking process and progress. Many ESL and EFL learner textbooks currently incorporate problem-solving and inquiry-based projects. Why, then, should teachers use technology? Keep in mind that if the technology does not make the language learning process more efficient or more effective, teachers should work to find more appropriate tools. As noted in the examples, however, computers can make language learning through inquiry and problem-solving more effective and more efficient by enabling learners to use language to develop multimedia presentations; to demonstrate ideas; to calculate, track, and organize; to access information to be transformed; and by facilitating a host of other tasks.

▶ Steps for Inquiry and Problem-Solving

Although problem-solving and inquiry are technically different, they require many of the same skills. At a minimum, students need to recognize the language that they will need and the processes involved. Critical thinking skills are also crucial for successful inquiry projects. Teachers can model some critical thinking skills, such as

- distinguishing fact from opinion
- assessing the reliability of a source
- assessing the accuracy of a statement
- distinguishing relevant from irrelevant information
- detecting bias
- identifying unstated assumptions
- recognizing logical inconsistencies (Hooper, Medeiros, & Smith, n.d.)

Critical thinking skills do not necessarily come naturally with second language learning, and they are culturally situated, so students need to learn and practice them before, during, and after each step in the process.

Although sources describe the steps in the inquiry process differently, most sources, such as the *Inquiry Page* (http://inquiry.uiuc.edu/), include the same five basic steps. These steps are addressed to the learner:

1. Ask a question that has meaning, define the problem, and figure out what you need to do to answer it.
2. Investigate by researching. Plan, gather resources and information, and record what you have found.
3. Create new ideas, thoughts, and directions for action. Make sense of the information you have gathered by summarizing, synthesizing, and interpreting.
4. Discuss with others. Interaction can shed new light on the question, the investigation, and the process. Share what you have learned and then use the feedback to return to the process.
5. Reflect on the inquiry process. Did the process lead to unexpected conclusions? Is there something else that needs researching? Has the problem been solved?

For younger or less proficient learners, Freeman and Freeman (1998) present six steps that follow these same basic guidelines. They call this the "Wonderfilled Way of Learning," and the steps are addressed to the teacher:

1. Ask the students: What do we know about _____?

2. Ask the students: What do we wonder about _____?
3. Ask the students: How can we find out about _____?
4. With the students, work out a plan of action, and, at the same time, work school district curriculum requirements into the unit.
5. Plan an event to celebrate what you have learned together.
6. Learning is continuous. From any unit, more topics and questions come up. Begin the cycle again. (pp. 138–139)

Regardless of which set of guidelines you and your students follow, inquiry projects can be used to support language and content learning.

In the chapter's opening scenario, Ms. Petrie guides the students through learning experiences. She has planned that throughout the project, they will not only learn techniques for inquiry such as planning, brainstorming, reflecting, and evaluating, but through their interactions, they will also acquire a variety of language content and structures. These activities facilitate many of the opportunities for effective language learning—for example, students have many opportunities for language input and production, they have many choices, they are motivated to learn because they are answering meaningful questions, and they interact with peers and community members. In many ways, such projects overlap with features of production (see chapter 5) because they enable students to produce creative results.

▶ Tips for Creating Opportunities for Inquiry and Problem-Solving

Two tips will help teachers develop effective CALL activities, particularly problem-solving and inquiry projects. First, teachers should never allow the tools to determine processes or products. In other words, they should first determine the language and project goals and structures, and then choose the appropriate tools, whether technology-based or not. Second, teachers need to help students fill individual roles and responsibilities within their groups so that each student has a reason to participate and to interact. These important tips will enable you to evaluate activities for problem-solving and inquiry.

▶ Activities for Inquiry and Problem-Solving

Currently, many language programs incorporate research classes, problem-solving activities, and other inquiry-based tasks into their curricula. Because students' cognitive development, more than their language ability, determines learner readiness to participate in inquiry, the examples presented below are divided into two grade-level categories: elementary and secondary/adult. General language and content objectives for these activities include learning and practicing vocabulary, pragmatics, and grammar such as forming questions and present tense; using descriptive language; scanning and skimming; and determining content and language needs for further study. In each category I provide one step-by-step example following the guidelines presented earlier and then provide descriptive summaries for other activities.

Elementary Examples

The Insect World

After several questions from K–2 students about why bees sting,

▶ **Ask the students:**

- What do we know about bugs? Students list the things they know—"They're icky," "They help plants," "Birds eat them," "They like picnics."

- What do we wonder about bugs? Students make another list—"Why do they sting?" "What do they eat?" "Why are there so many?" "Why don't they like cold weather?"

- How can we find out more about bugs? Work out a plan of action. For background information, facilitate their use of interactive multimedia Web sites such as *AntBoy's Bugworld* (Heater's World Productions, 1999) and *The Virtual Insectary* (http://www.virtualinsectary.com/), and crafts and activities from *Insects at Enchanted Learning* (EnchantedLearning.com, 2000). Be prepared to provide language or navigational support for students to understand and use these sites effectively. Students can also collect bugs, interview experts, or visit a local insectary.

Plan an event: Celebrate what you learned together. Perhaps go to an insect zoo where the learners are the docents and guides for other students.

Begin the cycle again: Revisit theme, using questions raised from this unit.

SimTown (n.v.)

▶ SimTown software enables students to build and maintain a town, and to ensure that the town thrives, they must balance resources, populations, and other factors. Unlike other Sim software packages, SimTown is appropriate for young children and does not contain adult situations or graphics. Each student in a team of four or so can play a role in this simulation—for example, a housing developer, a parks officer, a parent, a business owner. The software itself is basically free of language, so teachers and students have the opportunity to focus the language learning at the appropriate level and content.

GeoGame (Global SchoolNet Foundation, 2004a)

▶ This activity, from the Global Schoolhouse, offers two options for inquiry and problem-solving. In the first option, students are asked to "research information about your community, such as latitude, longitude, typical weather, land formations, time zone, population, points of interest, and for whom/what [it is] famous" (Global SchoolNet Foundation, 2004b). They then enter that information on the questionnaire provided on the Web site. The clues appear in a puzzle about the location that other students try to solve.

The second option is to play the GeoGame. To do so, students, "with help from maps, atlases, and other reference materials, match the description of each location in the game with the name of the corresponding city" (Global SchoolNet Foundation, 2004b). After the students have decided on their answers, they enter them into a form at the top of the game page. If all of the answers are correct, they receive a certificate.

The site provides suggestions for teachers, help for students, and choices of puzzles. During the process, learners are exposed to language input in many forms, and they can use skills that do not rely solely on language to accomplish their goal. However, because the goal is cooperative, students are encouraged to interact and negotiate as they proceed through the puzzle.

Education Place Project Center (Houghton Mifflin, 2004)

▶ Not all of the projects on this site involve inquiry or problem-solving, but many do, and they are focused on specific age and grade levels, which helps teachers to choose and adapt them for their classrooms. One interesting activity that requires students to reflect and research is *Movie in the Making* (Houghton Mifflin, 2001). The site explains the project this way:

> In this project students will report on a book by describing how they would turn that book into a motion picture. After reading and studying the main components of a novel (character, plot, conflict, climax and denouement), students will use their imaginations to explain how they would cast and direct the movie version. This project also provides enrichment activities wherein the students will access archived materials such as the Academy Awards Data Base, movie posters, and movie reviews. (Houghton Mifflin, 2001)

While students work to transform their knowledge from one format to another, this activity exposes them to a variety of language modes and genres, encourages them to be creative and thoughtful, and gives them an opportunity to produce their own brief movies using digital video equipment.

National Geographic Xpeditions (National Geographic Society, 2004)

▶ These Xpeditions are simple and use clear language, but the problems require thought and are perfect for group work. The National Geographic Society provides standards, lesson plans, resources, and tools to help teachers prepare and work with students as they solve the problem.

The *Crack the Code* activity requires students to problem-solve to figure out where the stolen goods are being taken. It presents a scenario in which the robbers dropped a clue that says

> First letters from each place-name read.
> Spell out the town and come with speed.

The note includes a number of other clues that turn out to be map coordinates. Instructions for solving the puzzle say

> [Using the coordinates,] (1) find those places in an atlas or on a map. (2) As you find each place, write its name next to the coordinates. (3) Circle the first letter of each name. (4) Read the letters from top to bottom, and they should spell the name of a city. Now you know where to nab those cartographic crooks. (National Geographic Society, 2003)

Answers to the puzzle are provided on the Web site. These Xpeditions are effective for language learning through globally focused content activities—the puzzle or game aspect makes them motivating. Learners interact with groups to plan and synthesize, and the Xpeditions Web site provides support to help students reach their goals.

Secondary/Adult Examples

Evaluating Web Sites

▶ **Ask:** How do I know if a Web site is trustworthy? Brainstorm definitions of *trustworthy*, reasons why trustworthiness is important, and how you might determine trustworthiness.

Investigate: Each team member should search the Web for sites that are questionable (urban legend sites are great for this) and for sites that suggest how to evaluate trustworthiness, or teachers can suggest or summarize sites, such as *Critically Analyzing Information Sources* (Engle & Cosgrave, 2004) at Cornell University.

Create: Summarize the data and make a *trustworthiness checklist*. Use the checklist to evaluate the questionable sites and come to some conclusions about them.

Discuss: Share the findings within the group and conduct further research as needed. Revise the checklist to satisfy any additional concerns. Reevaluate the original sites have others in the class evaluate sites using the checklist.

Reflect: Think about whether the solution answers the question sufficiently. If not, plan how to find a better answer.

This open-ended task encourages student language use and study as they voice their opinions, discuss current events, highlight their cultural foundations, explore the meaning of words, and create a useful product.

Solving History

▶ The *Discovery Channel* Web site (http://www.discovery .com/) presents globally focused "unsolved history" problems much like the National Geographic Xpeditions described earlier. A good example of one of these mysteries is *The Assassination of King Tut* (Discovery Communications, 2004). The site advances the theory that King Tut was murdered and claims that evidence is still available. It provides input from experts to shed light on the problems and solutions, a slide show, a photo tour, and clues for students to consider. When students have completed some of the examples, they can make their own locally focused unsolved history problems. Because it presents language in many different ways, the site is accessible to an array of students.

Grammar in Use

▶ Not all language programs present language through content, and certainly many students are interested in better understanding target language grammar. When students have questions about grammar, they have many ways to investigate answers and many resources to use. For example, students can use concordancing programs such as LinguaSys (Version 2.0), MonoConc Pro (Version 2.2), and Concordance (Watt, 2002) to gather and analyze authentic language data and draw their own conclusions (for more on concordancing, see Stevens, 1995). Learners can then share, explain, and compare their results with others. For students and programs that cannot afford to buy professional concordancing software, many other options are available, including the University of Illinois Linguacenter's *Grammar Safari* page (Mills & Salzmann, n.d.), which provides students with examples, a tutorial, and instructions on how to conduct grammar searches on the World Wide Web.

▶ Conclusion

Within the framework of inquiry, teachers should determine activities and tasks at least in part using students' questions. The examples in this chapter are specific examples of activities that can be carried out in myriad alternative ways. Even though learners enjoy the process of inquiry and problem-solving itself and find it motivating, effective language learning requires that the activities focus on language and content.

▶ Teachers' Voices

Another issue is documenting sources off the Internet. . . . I'm going to try using Microsoft Encarta Researcher. (It pulls the information off the site automatically and puts it in the proper format as students copy and paste the information into Researcher.) This should help students see the format . . . and help them realize you have to cite an Internet source just as you have to cite a book . . . .

Right before Thanksgiving I taught a signs/mapping/geography unit. It was a combination of life skills and English language learning. During this activity, one of my students told me a sad story. She said her father lived about 4 hours away, in Oregon, and she hadn't seen him in years and didn't feel confident driving down there. After practicing with an authentic map and learning more about street signs, she smiled a lot and said it really wasn't that hard. When we got back from break she told the class that she had, as a result of the class, driven down and visited with her father. This story inspired me and made me reflect on the lessons and activities and the impact they have, that I sometimes take for granted. The following quarter (that just ended), I took it one step further and showed students how to get into different Web sites that could not only provide maps, but also step-by-step directions, mileage, and even estimated time. They really enjoyed practicing planning trips and formulating presentations for the class with pictures of places they would visit. The exciting part was hearing their purpose for visiting places like Florida, California, and Arizona. Some were actually planning to visit family, and for others, it was a dream and a goal to take their children to Disneyland or other parts of this country.

All my students come from a culture of poverty. Often, within this culture, critical thinking isn't exposed, modeled, or taught. When I first began teaching my students to problem-solve in math, it was as if they had never activated a part of their brain. They don't take the time to reflect on what the question is actually asking; rather, they assume they know and blurt out a response that has nothing to do with the question. If it is true that "learning how to approach and solve problems, and accepting that there is often more than one answer to a question or more than one way of dealing with it, is a key part of both education and language learning," which I believe it is, then our language learners need to acquire, be taught, how to think critically. This type of higher level thinking doesn't occur in a vacuum. It must be systematically and repeatedly taught, modeled, and practiced. This skill will assist [English language] students not only in their language learning but in all academic areas.

I think as we reflect on cultural diversity in our classrooms, especially with ELLs [English language learners], it is important to provide opportunities for these students to learn in a style and manner that is fitting and conducive to them. Not all students think and solve problems in a linear fashion (from point A to B to C). Some students need to approach it from a different perspective, or a nonlinear approach.

chapter 7

Content-Based Instruction

▶ ## Focus

In this chapter you will

- learn about content-based instruction

- review the development of language objectives for content-based lessons

- reflect on the use of content-based software for language classrooms

A s you read the scenario, reflect on how using technology supports content and language learning in the project.

During her vacation, Ms. Peng, a middle school social studies teacher, completed the content based language teaching through technology (CoBaLTT) professional development modules (University of Minnesota, n.d.). She feels that what she learned will help her to teach content and language more effectively for her seventh graders, some of whom are English language learners. Ms. Peng wants to put this new information to use while she is designing lessons for her upcoming U.S. history course. The school curriculum specifies that the course should include studying U.S. pioneers, and Ms. Peng feels that technology can not only help her to address the students' content and language needs but also help them to have some authentic pioneer experiences. After she develops her objectives for both content and language for her unit on pioneer life, she decides to use a networked version of Broderbund's popular Oregon Trail software (5th edition) to supplement the textbook. To help students understand the issues and content necessary to have a successful journey on the Trail, she scans the museums on *MuseumLink's Museum of Museums* site (http://www .museumlink.com/) and finds a site provided by the National Museum of American History (Smithsonian Institution, 2002) where students use knowledge and logic to build a sod house, a common form of pioneer housing. To help her students reach the language objectives for the sod house lesson, Ms. Peng scans the graphic organizers available from North Central Regional Educational Laboratory (Learning Point Associates, 1988) and CoBaLTT (Cammarata, 2003). She decides that the "Decision-Maker's Flow Chart" (Cammarata, 2003) will support student language during the sod house exercise by integrating a writing component, scaffolding group discussion, and encouraging students to use lesson-compatible language. Although Ms. Peng will not use technology for all of her lessons, she feels that technology will help her learners stay engaged in pioneer life and meet the unit's objectives.

► Overview of Content-Based Instruction

Other chapters in this book have touched on the use of content-based software and Web sites to support learning activities such as inquiry, production, and communication. This chapter focuses on using content-based technologies for content and language learning. Content-based language instruction (also known by many other names, e.g., *content-centered instruction*) attempts to meet students' needs in both content and language, and it can occur in both language and content (at the elementary school level called *mainstream*) classes. There are variations on the theme, ranging from using content area texts and materials to offering adjunct language support courses along with the content courses, to providing theme-based or sheltered language courses. In content-based language learning classrooms, content is purposeful, not just a vehicle to learn language; rather, the language is the vehicle for content learning (Crandall, 1994). In other words, content area teachers and language teachers need to learn some of each other's expertise so that they can not only meet their students' needs but also successfully work together in doing so.

Language teachers have many reasons to focus on content. Because each content area has its own jargon, culture, and methods and employs language structures in specific ways, language plays an essential role in content learning. In addition, as Crandall (1994) mentions, content makes tasks meaningful, authentic, and accessible to learners. It also helps them to acquire academic language proficiency while learning language, rather than having to learn the language first and then learning academic concepts (Cummins, 1999). Furthermore, each content area has its own standards (see ISTE, 2002a), and the sooner learners begin working toward these standards, the more they can achieve. During her unit on pioneer life, for example, Ms. Peng is working toward these social studies standards for middle grades while she is teaching the language needed to reach them:

- Describe how people create places that reflect cultural values and ideals as they build neighborhoods, parks, shopping centers, and the like.
- Examine, interpret, and analyze physical and cultural patterns and their interactions, such as land use, settlement patterns, cultural transmission of customs and ideas, and ecosystem changes.
- Describe how historical events have been influenced by, and have influenced, physical and human geographic factors in local, regional, national, and global settings. (National Council for the Social Studies, 1994)

Ms. Peng is still working within the conditions for optimal language learning environments while she develops her content goals. The ultimate goal of integrating content and language is to help students become academically proficient with the content of the discipline.

▶ Supporting Content-Based Language Instruction

The literature on content-based instruction includes many ideas for how to support both language and content learning. Below are two especially important techniques.

1. **Teach content in a culturally responsive manner.**

   Teaching in a culturally responsive manner means using literature that is culturally relevant (Echevarria & Graves, 2002), using first language cognates where it helps student comprehension, and adapting lessons to reflect the contributions of all relevant groups. For example, Mexicans, Puerto Ricans, and people of other backgrounds and nationalities fought for the United States during World War II, and lessons on the war should reflect this diversity. Web and software resources can help teachers be culturally responsive by allowing them to access culturally relevant information quickly when needed; these resources may also suggest places to include such information that the teacher might not have considered. Using software to make family connections (as suggested in chapter 10) can also help teachers understand learners' cultural resources. As part of the unit described in this chapter's opening scenario, Ms. Peng will include culturally relevant material in each lesson; for example, she will address who the pioneers were, where they came from, what contributions they made, and also what problems they caused.

2. **Adapt materials so that they are appropriate for learners, but do not sacrifice academic content.**

   To make materials more accessible to students, Echevarria and Graves (2002) suggest that teachers

   - use graphic depiction
   - outline the text
   - rewrite the text
   - use audiotapes
   - provide live demonstrations
   - use alternate books

It is important, in addition, that the grammatical structures in the adapted materials include the types of structures found in the original text.

Teachers do not have to make all of these changes themselves—they can enlist more proficient students to help, work in teacher groups and share materials, and find many of these materials already posted to the Web.

▶ Tips for Designing Content-Based Language Instruction

In addition to the two techniques just mentioned, an important skill for teachers to develop is the ability to create measurable objectives that address both language and content. The literature provides suggestions for how this may be done, and many tools exist for this purpose. One of the most useful is Short and Echevarria's (1999) *The Sheltered Instruction Observation Protocol,* which helps to develop content-based language instruction by providing a thorough and pedagogically sound set of criteria. Another useful tool is the lesson plan outline used in the CoBaLTT project database (Johnshoy, 2001). Each plan lists objectives for content and culture and then breaks language objectives into two categories: content obligatory, which students must use to complete the lesson, and content compatible, which are related language objectives that students can focus on. The lessons also include objectives for strategies and social development. To this set of objectives teachers can also add technology objectives that meet technology standards. In short, whether teachers formally document what their students need to learn using these tools or use a less formal system, teachers of content-based language lessons must keep in mind both content and language objectives.

▶ Examples of Using Content, Language, and Technology Objectives

Language teachers may have difficulty setting content objectives, and content teachers may have difficulty setting language objectives. For this reason, among others, language and content teachers should coordinate their instruction and cooperate in developing objectives. Finding lessons on the Web that have objectives outlined can also facilitate this process, as can practice developing objectives.

Examples of content and language objectives for CALL lessons follow; these examples also integrate sample content-area standards. The sample activity included in each example suggests technologies that may be used to meet the objectives. Although not specifically mentioned here, each lesson is developed with the conditions for learning (chapter 1) in mind.

Content Area: Science

Objectives

▶ **Content:** Identify simple machines, understand and apply the equation *force* x *distance* = *work,* understand the relationship of force and distance to work, set up an experiment, and observe and chart the mechanical advantage gained from using simple machines. (Some of the objectives are taken from the teacher's guide for the Science Court: Work and Simple Machines, Version 1.0.3 software mentioned later.)

Language: *Content Obligatory:* Define and use with increasing accuracy these words: *work, force/effort force, mechanical advantage, simple machine.* Use present tense to describe events that happen regularly. Predict, summarize, listen for facts, exemplify. *Content Compatible:* Participate comfortably in discussion, use appropriate turn-taking, ask questions, and disagree politely.

Standards: National Academy of Sciences (1996)

Goal: A1. Abilities necessary to do scientific inquiry:

• ask a question about objects, organisms, and events in the environment

• plan and conduct a simple investigation

• employ simple equipment and tools to gather data and extend the senses

• use data to construct a reasonable explanation

• communicate investigations and explanations

Sample Activity

During this lesson, the learners participate in multimedia tasks presented in the Science Court: Work and Simple Machines software (Version 1.0.3) and accompanying external documents. The software presents cartoon video footage of a four-part trial in which scientific knowledge determines the outcomes. Students work in cooperative groups to collect data, answer questions, make predictions, and demonstrate understanding of the concepts presented.

Content Area: Mathematics

Objectives

▶ **Content:** Choose appropriate arithmetic operations, compute answers, communicate about math, perform multistep problems with multiple operations, estimate, and present mathematical ideas orally.

Language: *Content Obligatory:* Define and use with increasing accuracy the following vocabulary: *number, step, unit, multiply, divide, add, subtract, quantity.* Use past tense to describe orally and in writing mathematical processes (e.g., I took 10 away from *b* and divided by *a*). Understand and follow the steps in the problem-solving process. Watch and listen for essential information, take accurate notes, and explain mathematical answers orally and in writing without using numbers. *Content Compatible:* Use appropriate group processes, demonstrate accurate subject and verb agreement (e.g., She tooks, no she *took*, the money to the bank), demonstrate accurate number agreement, express reasons for choices, and construct simple sentences.

Standards: National Council of Teachers of Mathematics (1998)

Standard 6: Problem-solving. Mathematics instructional programs should focus on solving problems as part of understanding mathematics so that
all students

- build new mathematical knowledge through their work with problems

- develop a disposition to formulate, represent, abstract, and generalize in situations within and outside mathematics

- apply a wide variety of strategies to solve problems and adapt the strategies to new situations

- monitor and reflect on their mathematical thinking in solving problems

Standard 8: Communication. Mathematics instructional programs should use communication to foster understanding of mathematics so that all students

- organize and consolidate their mathematical thinking to communicate with others

- express mathematical ideas coherently and clearly to peers, teachers, and others

- extend their mathematical knowledge by considering the thinking and strategies of others

- use the language of mathematics as a precise means of mathematical expression

Sample Activity

As part of this lesson, learners complete tasks presented in the software package Fizz and Martina's Math Adventure: Project Sphinx (Version 3.3). Much like with the Science Court software, Math Adventure presents students with a set of multimedia scenarios during which they must note and use mathematical data to help their team solve the characters' problems.

Content Areas: Geography, Social Studies, Mathematics

Objectives

▶ **Content:** Use trial and error to develop a balanced town ecology; research facts related to decisions; track, record, and report on processes and outcomes; and explain outcomes in terms of geography, culture, quantity, and so on.

Language: *Content Obligatory:* Define and use with increasing accuracy the following vocabulary: *town, city, goods and services, balance, development, costs, pollution, quantity, description, data, pattern, ecology, housing, resident, labor.* Express and support opinions. Indicate agreement and disagreement. *Content Compatible:* Use descriptive words (e.g., *big, small, extra, difficult*) appropriately, use past tense to describe group processes (e.g., We agreed to add the school), and make suggestions.

Standards: National Council for the Social Sciences (1994); Qualifications and Curriculum Authority (2001)

Attainment level: knowledge and understanding of environmental change and sustainable development

Sample Activity

SimTown (n.v.), mentioned previously, is a virtually text-free simulation that allows users to build a town from the ground up, succeeding or failing based on the balance that they achieve among all the important components. In cooperative groups, learners make decisions about what to add to the town, why to add it, and where it should be placed. Group members must research successes and failures in other forums and explain the outcomes.

Content Area: Music

Objectives

► **Content:** Listen to and choose music appropriate to a chosen culture, explain the music chosen, use authentic personal materials from the target culture to support ideas or issues, research ideas and issues, choose key concepts related to music, and summarize and present in a multimedia project.

Language: *Content Obligatory:* List vocabulary relevant to topic, use present tense to describe everyday events, take notes from authentic sources, and use comprehensible pronunciation during presentation. *Content Compatible:* Use pronouns appropriately (e.g., instruments as *it* or *they* rather than *he* or *she*), use article/noun agreement accurately (e.g., *a flute, some* instruments), and use and explain phrases and idioms appropriate to the target culture.

Standards: National Association for Music Education (n.d.)

Standard 6: listening to, analyzing, and describing music

Standard 9: understanding music in relation to history and culture

> *Sample Activity*
>
> Using any of the many multimedia tools available, learners create a presentation that presents an overview of the music of a chosen culture, preferably one with which they are familiar or have had experience.

▶ Tools for Content-Based Technology

Many Web sites and software programs emphasize content learning in effective and authentic ways, from the global *Cable News Network* (http://www.cnn.com/) and the *U.S. National Aeronautics and Space Administration* (http://www.nasa.gov) to Encarta (n.v.) and Sammy's Science House (Version 1.4), and many more can support content-based learning, such as PowerPoint, FrontPage, and other multimedia development packages. However, many language educators ask whether commercial software and Web sites intended for native-speaking audiences can or should be used in language classrooms.

The answer is that teachers should use such software and Web sites only when they have carefully planned how to use them so that they meet the conditions for effective language learning (chapter 1). Meeting those conditions means, in part, that teachers have provided any necessary organizers, prompts, or adaptations to make the language and content accessible to the students; that the content and language are relevant and authentic; and that the objectives for the language and content are clear. If these conditions are met, the technology's multimedia-multimodal-nonlinear presentation of information will probably result in more gains than losses.

▶ Conclusion

Content cannot be learned without language, and even language can serve as content for lessons. In addition, learners usually demonstrate understanding of content by using language, and they demonstrate language learning by discussing or writing about content. In other words, the relationship between language and content is both receptive and active. Because the two are intertwined, CALL teachers need to be mindful of the difficulties that learners can face in meeting both language and content objectives, particularly if these objectives are not made explicit. Teaching in a culturally responsive manner, including making sure that software and Web sites do not present unexplored biases, can help learners achieve in both language and content areas.

▶ Teachers' Voices

I like PBS and National Geographic for the multimedia presentation they offer, lesson plans recommended, connection to television shows, and the variety of themes to represent.

I always provide students with books, encyclopedias, atlases, magazines to conduct research as well as Web sites, Encarta, McNally Atlas CD. Some of us still prefer written material we can touch, quickly refer back to. I find that when I read longer materials on the computer that I tend to click on links and eventually lose my original place.

I really enjoyed this Web site and wanted to emphasize it to all of you. The Web site is www.nationalgeographic.com; go into the NG Kids [section]. I found some exciting experiments that our students could do at home with materials they would all have access to. Also they can be performed in class if you choose. This site has a lot for all ages. The graphics are wonderful and the feature stories are very engaging. There are contests, jokes, and many links. I hope you find it as rewarding for our ELLs (and all other students) as I did.

I know this is way above pre-primer, but I was really amazed to find that Encarta has a read-aloud option. What is cool is that you can change the pitch of the computerized voice (so it sounds more like a man's or a woman's voice), and you can change the speed, so it can read really slow. You can read selected parts of the text or the whole thing. I wish I had known about this earlier. I have not used all aspects of Encarta with many of my kids, because the reading level is too high; however, I think a lot (but not all!) could listen to it and get something out of it.

I have found that multimedia authoring software, for me, is time consuming and not always the best use of my time. . . . Granted that authoring software is more flexible; I just do not know if the time investment is always worth it. My students have used PowerPoint, Excel spreadsheet for graphs [and] data; we have a class scanner, a digital camera, [color] printer. Students use the technology for their research projects. I always provide specific Web sites they may use for their research—otherwise they are all over the place and never find the needed information.

The cover story in April, 2003, *NEA Today* is about computers and technology. You can access the article at http://www.nea.org/neatoday /0304/cover.html. The things they are doing in regular classrooms is awesome—animate long division problems, diagram the parts of a cell, complete a spelling quiz their teacher "beams" to them . . . WOW.

chapter 8

▶ **Assessment**

▶ Focus

In this chapter you will

- reflect on the uses of assessment in CALL classrooms
- examine guidelines and techniques for authentic assessment
- explore other issues of assessment

As you read the anecdote below, reflect on the guidelines for assessment that the teacher is following.

English language learners in Ms. Hagerty's seventh- and eighth-grade class are working on the design of historical books that they will then produce using Edmark's Imagination Express Destination: Time Trip USA (Version 1.1) software package. Student teams have each chosen a figure from U.S. history to research and about whom they will construct a first-person narrative. The goal is to distill the most useful and important facts about the figure's life. Each book will be a minimum of five pages long and will include text, graphics, and narration. Each project must use as resources at least three books, two Web sites (with justification for accuracy of the materials), and one other resource. After deciding which tasks the activity will involve, team members divide the tasks among themselves.

As team members work individually or together to complete their tasks, Ms. Hagerty walks around the room, observing, asking questions, and providing feedback when necessary. She notices that communication for one team has broken down, and she facilitates a discussion that helps the members get back on track. One student searching for information on the Web about her team's character seems to be stymied by the number of hits she has received in her electronic search, so the teacher helps the student reflect on how she might solve this problem. At the end of the class period, Ms. Hagerty asks students to comment on any problems that they had, how they progressed during the period, and what their plan is for completing the project. She also asks them to write several sentences about what they have learned about the figure they are investigating.

▶ Overview of Assessment in Language Learning

Assessment is one of the most important aspects of language teaching and learning. Assessment has two main purposes: to make summative evaluations and to provide instructional feedback to help learners progress. Both summative and formative assessments can be formal (standardized) or informal (classroom-based). Informally, assessment provides feedback from peers and others; formally, it provides information against a standard about how the student is progressing in specific areas. Everyone can be involved in assessment—peers, teacher, self, administrators, and external constituents.

Assessment supports the conditions for language learning if it is interactive, formative, and authentic.

Although standardized testing has become increasingly more intrusive for language teachers, much has been written and continues to be written about this topic; therefore, in this chapter we address classroom-based assessments. As Chao (1999) discussed in *CALL Environments,* regardless of whether language, content, tool use, or some other aspect of learning in CALL classrooms is being assessed, teachers need to make classroom-based assessments authentic. Generally, Chao explained that such assessments help learners

- move ahead and improve
- gain familiarity with content being taught
- become aware of their own position in the language learning process
- fine-tune their understanding of the target language and culture
- set goals for the next stage of learning (p. 244)

Clearly, these are fundamental goals for learners because they support intentional cognition and achievement. In *CALL Environments* (1999), I note that teachers must also focus on authentic assessments that

- take place in multiple contexts
- assess both process and outcomes
- are spread out over time
- fit the content and method of what is taught (p. 258)

This last guideline may be the most difficult to implement. It means, for example, that grammar learned in context should not be tested out of context, and that science content knowledge acquired through experimenting should be assessed in the same situation. Chao (1999) adds that teachers should use assessments that are learner centered, integrated into classroom activity, and encourage students to reflect and learn consciously. In *CALL Environments* (1999), I describe examples of authentic assessment techniques such as verbal reporting, observation, retelling, graphic organizers, role-plays, journals, portfolios, and self-assessment. Although these guidelines and examples may make the assessment process in language classrooms seem rather simple, in reality it can be quite complex. This is particularly true for CALL classrooms, where technology use may be an additional factor in the assessment.

How are computers used in assessment in CALL classrooms? Generally they are used in two ways. First, computers are used to perform the actual assessment or to help carry out assessment. For example, some CALL software programs can assess learners based on the number of questions they answer correctly. In addition, computers can help in assessment by allowing learners to post their products to the Web for feedback or send their output electronically to experts to evaluate. Comments from external evaluators can then be counted for part of the project grade. Furthermore, the computer can be used to create rubrics and record observations and reflections. They can also help teachers and students keep a running total of points earned and function as a tool during assessments to help the teacher record, weigh, summarize, and report on student progress. Examples of commonly used assessment tools include computer-based tests (described later in this chapter), spreadsheets, grading programs, test-making software (e.g., Essential Teacher Tools, Version 1.2), and rubric-making software (e.g., Schrock, 2003; Teachnology, 2003).

Second, teachers assess the product and process of the students' work with and through the computer. In other words, computer-enhanced tasks that students complete and the work processes that they use while completing the tasks can be assessed. (Unless the goal of the task is to learn computer skills, such skills should not be a focus of assessment.) The assessment focus is the same as that for language learning tasks that are produced with other tools. However, because CALL projects may have multiple components (sound, visuals, text, graphics, etc.), assessing a multimedia presentation developed in a team may require the teacher to consider and evaluate criteria that would not be used to evaluate a printed essay. (This idea is discussed in more depth in the section on rubrics.)

In this chapter's opening scenario, while students work on their CALL project, Ms. Hagerty uses many informal assessments to evaluate her language learners' language and content processes. She observes, discusses, and encourages students to reflect on both process and product. Later in the project, she and her learners will develop a rubric for evaluating the project outcomes and an assessment for measuring content and language gains.

▶ Tips for Developing Assessments

The guidelines for assessing language learning activities in CALL classrooms are no different from those for assessing them in other contexts. For example, like Ms. Hagerty, teachers should involve students in the development of assessments. Involving students not only exposes them to more language and content and provides a deeper understanding about expectations for the activity, but it also helps them to develop metacognitive awareness about assessment. Throughout this book, I have advocated developing such awareness for all aspects of language learning, and it is equally important for assessment.

Although authentic assessments are the ideal, language students are typically involved in plenty of standardized testing, both large scale (region, state, or nationwide) and small scale (classroom or program based). To help them develop metacognitive awareness and practice cognitive strategies for learning and assessment, students can find software packages, such as SemNet (n.v.), and Web sites, such as the Test of English as a Foreign Language (n.v., see ETS, 2004). Readers will also find many good texts and articles to assist them with strategies in specific areas such as reading or grammar learning. However, few of these resources are accessible to language learners of different levels or include strategies and exercises that are generalizable to content outside of the text or software.

One exception is Brain Cogs (n.v.), developed by Fablevision and the Institute for Learning and Development and Research. Brain Cogs is a software program accompanied by related materials to help learners learn, reflect on, and use specific strategies (see Figure 8.1). Although developed for a native-English-speaking audience, the multimedia presentation and accompanying scaffolds make it effective for learners with low-intermediate or higher English language proficiency.

The software uses a narrative about a rock band, the Rotten Green Peppers, to demonstrate the five *cogs*: *remembering, organizing information, prioritizing, shifting perspectives,* and *checking for mistakes.* An accompanying video contains animations from the program, making it possible for the teacher to work with learners on the concepts before they use the software. As learners see the band working through the cogs in the software, they also learn strategies to apply in their own lives and work; each of the 13 strategies that are part of the five cogs can be applied across content and language areas and are useful before, during, and after tests. The exercises are entertaining and employ sound, text, and graphics in creative ways.

The software contains printouts for students to use as support and a tracking and scoring system that can show instructors not only which strategies work for their students but also which they need to address more thoroughly. As important as the content and motivational features, the software is multiculturally appropriate, clearly suggests ways for teachers to

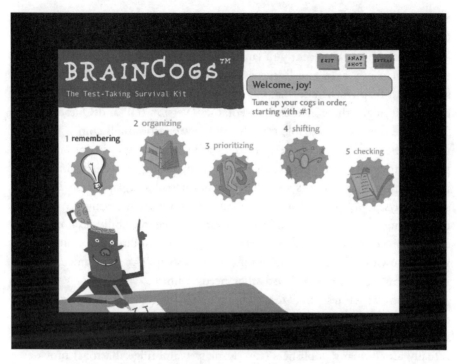

Figure 8.1. The five cogs from BrainCogs.

work as a cognitive coach for students, and contains rewards that directly relate to the strategies. Instructors can use the accompanying posters to preteach vocabulary and ideas and to remind students of the strategies. For screenshots and more information about the program, visit the FableVision Shoppe (http://www.fablevision.com/).

Whether using software or other materials, teachers need to follow the assessment guidelines to effectively assess student progress and push students to higher achievement.

▶ Tools for Assessment

Crucial to the assessment process is preparing students to take tests and helping them to participate in their own assessment. Teachers have many resources and tools available, both electronic and paper based, to meet these objectives. One tool is computerized testing, and a useful resource is the rubric.

Computerized Testing

Computer-based testing (CBT) and computer-adaptive testing (CAT) have become more popular recently in language assessment. CBT presents items to the test taker in a fixed and linear fashion. Many software programs are available to help teachers format CBT tests and to save test content in different formats; these include Hot Potatoes (Version 6.0) and Question Tools (free download available from http://www.questiontools.com/). CAT, on the other hand, presents items to the learner according to his or her previous answers and response patterns, individualizing the assessment process. Computerized tests are different from pencil-and-paper tests in several ways. Dunkel (n.d.) notes that using computerized testing "saves testing time and decreases examinee frustration since low-ability examinees are not forced to take test items constructed for high-ability testees, and vice versa." Brown (1997) adds that computerized tests do not need proctors, so students can take as much time as they need to finish.

However, such tests may test computer skills in addition to (or exclusive of) language skills (Kirsch, Taylor, Jamieson, & Eignor, 1998). Students should therefore practice using computerized testing programs before they are actually tested; many publishers (e.g., Kaplan, Cambridge, Barrons) provide practice tests and tips. Brown (1997), however, raises a number of concerns about CBT in general, such as limited screen capacity and poor graphics capabilities. Alderson, Clapham, and Wall (1995) suggest that developers of placement, progress, achievement, proficiency, and diagnostic tests specify exactly what abilities the tests are measuring, what test methods are being employed, and what scoring and evaluation criteria are being used (p. 19). This information will better enable teachers to use computerized tests for language classrooms to meet the goals for authentic assessment and optimal language learning experiences.

Using Rubrics for Assessment

As academic standards become more specific and demands for implementation more strident, many language and content educators are designing rubrics, and having their students design rubrics, to evaluate student achievement. Pickett and Dodge (2001) note that

> rubrics can be created in a variety of forms and levels of complexity;
> however, they all contain common features which
> • focus on measuring a stated objective (performance, behavior, or quality)

- use a range to rate performance
- contain specific performance characteristics arranged in levels indicating the degree to which a standard has been met

Pickett and Dodge add that using rubrics in assessment offers certain advantage. They

- enable more objective and consistent assessment
- force the teacher to clarify his/her criteria in specific terms
- clearly show the students what is expected and how their work will be evaluated
- promote student awareness of the criteria to use in assessing peer performance
- provide useful feedback regarding the effectiveness of the instruction
- provide benchmarks against which to measure and document progress

Developing good rubrics takes time and practice, but these benefits make them useful and effective assessment tools in CALL classrooms.

Designing Rubrics for CALL Activities

Many educators find it difficult to design effective rubrics at first, but tools are available to help. For example, rubric generators, such as Teachnology's project rubric generator (Teachnology, 2003), format the information quickly and easily. Whether teachers use a rubric generator or type their rubric in a word processing program, however, the decision steps are the same and teachers must supply the rubric's content. Following these general steps can help teachers to ensure a successful assessment process.

- Review goals and objectives for the project or task.
- Think about what an efficient and effective process would look like and how it meets the goals. Think about what an excellent finished product would look like (and how it would meet the goals). Note what aspects of the goals that the process and the product meet and how they do so.
- Decide on major categories for assessment. Check these against the goals and the finished project description to make sure that you have not left out any important categories.
- Develop subcategories as needed. For example, if one of your categories is "uses technology appropriately," you might want to include a subcategory dealing with ethical use.
- Divide your scale appropriately. Thinking of descriptions for more than five numbers takes a great deal of time and effort, so many rubrics have

multiple point options for each criteria within a category (e.g., 1–2, 3–4, 5–6) or a simple five-point scale for each category. It is important that students know the relative importance or weight of all of the subcategories.

- Develop precise descriptions for each ranking in your scale. The use of quantifiable elements helps students understand minimums for each level. If you use words like *kind of, rarely,* and so on, give examples of how the scoring of each ranking looks in practice.
- Review the rubric according to the guidelines outlined previously. For example, ask yourself, "Is the assessment authentic? Learner centered? Integrated into classroom activity? Does it take place in multiple contexts, assess both process and outcomes, fit the content and method of what is taught, and encourage students to reflect and learn consciously?" If the rubric does not meet these goals, revise or choose another form of assessment.
- Use the rubric.
- Revise the rubric after using it. Teachers can also revise in progress if it becomes clear that the rubric is not fair or that something has been left out. Just be sure the students know what the changes are and why they were made.

A rubric for Ms. Hagerty's project in the opening scenario could take many different forms. The following is one example of how she might complete each of the steps.

Project: Historical Book

▶ **Goals and objectives:** Work with teammates effectively, distinguish fact from fiction, learn historical facts, use past tense, practice narrative format, produce error-free text (grammar and spelling), follow instructions, and meet standards in social studies and ESL.

Process, product: An effective process has students working together to find answers to questions, dividing work so everyone does an equitable (not necessarily equal) share, completing tasks on time, using technology efficiently, and working in English as much as possible. An excellent product would be creative, well illustrated, free of grammatical errors, factually correct, in narrative format, and complete; have clear audio; and share important historical information about the figure.

Major categories: process, product

Subcategories: *Process:* division of work, completion of tasks, use of technology, use of English, teamwork. *Product:* completeness, format, content, creativity, comprehensibility.

Scale divisions: 1–5 for each subcategory (total of 50 points)

Descriptions: General levels are

1 = does not meet the goal

2 = somewhat meets the goal

3 = almost meets the goal

4 = clearly meets the goal

5 = exceeds the goal

A finished rubric for the project could look something like Figure 8.2 (see pp. 128–129).

Rubrics do not stand alone in classrooms. Ms. Hagerty will review this rubric with her students several times, answering questions about the evaluation (including explaining any terms that they do not understand), updating students on their team's progress according to the rubric as she observes their work, and using the rubric as a framework through which to discuss the project.

▶ Conclusion

Issues of testing and other assessment are often controversial. Clearly, developing and implementing effective assessments is a difficult task. By following guidelines and focusing on goals, however, teachers can make sure that the assessments are useful learning experiences for all involved.

▶ Teachers' Voices

At my school, when we display student work, a rubric must also be displayed (tied to Essential Academic Learning Standards or district

	1	2	3	4	5
Process Division of work	Work was not divided equitably. Team members did not agree on divisions, some members did not do any work. Most team members are dissatisfied.	Work was divided somewhat equitably, but several team members did more than others. Some team members are dissatisfied.	Work was divided fairly equitably. Most team members are satisfied.	Work was divided equitably. Team members are satisfied.	Work was divided very equitably, all team members agree and would work this way again.
Completion of tasks	No tasks were completed in a timely manner.	At least 50% of the tasks were done on time.	At least 80% of the tasks were done on time.	All tasks were completed on time.	All tasks were completed in a timely manner, some were done early.
Use of technology	Technology was not used efficiently. Team members wasted time surfing, preparing irrelevant graphics or sound, or just fooling around.	Technology use was only somewhat efficient. Team members sometimes viewed unrelated sites and were off topic.	Technology use was fairly efficient. Team members used their time on the computer fairly wisely.	Technology use was focused and efficient.	Technology was used very efficiently to find answers and obtain and develop content.
Use of English	English was used less than 70% of the time.	English was used 70% of the time.	English was used 80% of the time.	English was used 90% of the time.	English was used nearly 100% of the time.
Teamwork	Teamwork was not efficient. Questions were not answered by the group. Time was wasted.	Some team members were on task. Some questions were answered by the team.	Most team members were on task. Most questions were answered by the team.	All team members were on task. Most questions were answered by team members.	All team members were on task constantly. Questions were answered by the team. Team exhibited exemplary teamwork.
Product Completeness	The product was very incomplete. It was missing either parts of all components or one whole component (5 pages, text, audio, 5 facts, or graphics).	The product was incomplete. It was missing parts of two or more com-ponents.	The product was almost complete but missing part of one component.	The product was complete (5 pages, audio, graphics, 5 facts and text).	The product was complete and at least one extra component was added.

Format	Product was not in narrative format. Illustrations and audio did not contribute to the story. Past tense was not used.	Product was partly in narrative format. Illustrations and audio were only somewhat relevant. Past tense was used in part.	Product was mostly in narrative format. Illustrations and audio were mostly relevant. Past tense was used inconsistently.	Product was in narrative format. Illustrations and audio contributed to the story. Past tense was used consistently.	Product was in correct first person narrative format. Illustrations and audio were vital to the story. Past tense was used correctly throughout.
Comprehensibility	5 or more grammar and/or spelling mistakes and/or audio or text was unintelligible. The story did not make sense.	4 or more grammar and/or spelling mistakes and/or audio or text was only partly intelligible.	3 or more grammar and/or spelling mistakes and/or audio or text was mostly intelligible. Most of the story made sense.	1 or more grammar and/or spelling mistakes and/or audio or text was intelligible. The story made sense.	No grammar or spelling mistakes. Text and audio were very clear. The story was well-written and easy to understand.
Content	Many factual errors. Many facts were peripheral to the story. Graphics were superfluous. Audio did not add to the story.	Some factual errors. Some facts were peripheral to the story. Much of the graphics and audio were irrelevant.	A few factual errors. One or more facts were peripheral to the story. Some of the graphics and audio were irrelevant.	One factual error. All facts were central to the story. Graphics and audio were relevant.	No factual errors. All facts used were central to the story. Graphics were extremely relevant and audio was necessary to the story.
Creativity	The story was not creative. The use of graphics, text, and sound was not creative.	The story was somewhat creative. Sounds, text, and graphics were not used very creatively.	The story was fairly creative. Sound, text, and graphics were used in fairly creative ways.	The story was creative. Sound, text, and graphics were used in some creative ways.	The story was very creative. Sound, text, and graphics were used creatively.

Figure 8.2. Possible rubric for the project.

curriculum learning goals). Our assistant principal introduced Rubistar—great tool. You may use the rubric as provided or customize your own. What we have found at our school is that those of us using Rubistar are now better at writing/creating our own rubrics and aligning the expectations/assessment with the learning goals.

This can be a part of a reading unit. After students read several books, they can choose a favorite theme or quote from a story and design it in Photoshop. Once the design is complete, they can print this on t-shirt paper and then iron the design on t-shirts. This is a fun way to evaluate their understanding of some themes or quotes from books.

Educational assessment should follow the principles of integration, autonomy, guiding, critical thinking, and process as well as product. My sixth graders are still mastering the keyboard; therefore, any assessment must take into consideration their lack of keyboard experience. The reading assessment we use at our school requires students to type a one-letter response to comprehension questions. I have noticed some students are taking up precious seconds looking for the correct letter (limited to a, b, c, d). I am thinking of somehow highlighting these letters for them. Would this be considered cheating?

I have used role-plays in the past with my adult ESL students. Usually I used them at the end of a unit on health or jobs. Students role-played going to the emergency room or a doctor's appointment. Also we role-play interviewing for a job and in other units as well. I realize that it is a good idea to use role-playing to assess prior knowledge (at the beginning of a unit) and for identifying any gaps in content knowledge. This type of assessment would be a good indicator for me as the teacher as well as for my students on what knowledge, both concept and vocabulary needs, exists. It would also drive my lessons and make my instruction more intentional and focused on what my students would really benefit from.

The whole concept of learner autonomy in assessment is news to me. As far as I was concerned, state, administrators, and teachers had the only say in how to assess students. I've now learned that portfolios, peer reviews, and self-assessments can empower and motivate the students. But I do agree that empowering students is not an easy thing to do because learner and teacher must both change their attitudes and the way they interact with each other. Learner autonomy: Wow, what a concept!

Most assessments that are computer created and taken on the computer are fill-in-the-blank, multiple-choice, true-false. I have used the Web site FunBrain for these types of "tests" and the kids are motivated to do well. FunBrain sends me the results (I do not have to grade) with comments about which questions most students missed. There is a section for essay, but I would have to assess. Essays and other critical thinking assessments are possible on the computer; however, my students' typing skills are limited— and time becomes a factor. Our school uses a reading and math computer-based assessment. Again students have to make a choice from the offered selection. But, the program monitors their reading speed and level—adjusts the difficulty of the reading materials, provides in-depth reports for teachers/parents about strengths/weaknesses and strategies/suggestions on how to help the student improve. This is just an additional assessment tool and we do not use it as the only tool.

I am not really the expert in electronic portfolios but a friend of mine uses them with her second graders and has great results. She uses electronic portfolios created out of a program called The Portfolio Assessment Tool Kit. I intend to set this up for my first-grade students next year and have it follow their progress till fourth grade.

chapter9

Limitations, Caveats, and Challenges

► Focus

In this chapter you will

- consider how new literacies, differently abled students, limited technology contexts, culture and the law influence student achievement

- consider suggestions for working through the challenges

- reflect on the gains and losses that using technology brings in the classroom

As you read the following scenario, think about influences on student achievement in technology-supported language classrooms.

Ms. Johnston had carefully planned the activity for her lab time with her fifth grade students, making sure that each had a role to play, knew what to do and how to do it, and was aware of the goals of the activity and how to obtain feedback. Although this was the students' first time in the lab, Ms. Johnston expected a successful experience because she had set up the environment so carefully.

Once in the lab, Ms. Johnston set the students to work. Although some of the students jumped right in, Dari and Stephen were very confused about the array of buttons, instructions, and windows on their screen and could not figure out how to begin. Jana, who had a visual impairment, could not read the text on the screen, and Alice, who was physically challenged, had a difficult time using the mouse. Anu politely but firmly declined to work on the computer; Ms. Johnston did not understand Anu's obstinacy until she later discovered that Anu's father did not believe that computers were an appropriate part of schooling and did not want her to participate in such activities. Many of the students completed their tasks successfully, but Ms. Johnston was concerned that she had failed to address the needs of all her students and determined to work more attentively toward this goal.

▶ Overview of Factors That Influence Student Achievement

Although Ms. Johnston based her lab activities on principles for effective CALL, she did not consider other factors in the environment that could have an impact on student outcomes. This is not surprising—although computers can be used as a tool in the same ways that pencil and paper can, they are capable of more than such tools, and both learners and teachers must understand both the advantages and liabilities of using computers. This chapter focuses briefly on five areas for reflection: new literacies, the needs of differently abled students, computer uses in limited technology contexts, the impacts of culture in CALL classrooms, and legal issues of technology use.

▶ Teaching New Literacies

If you type the word *literacies* into your word processor, the software will probably mark it as incorrect in spelling or grammar; however, literacies is becoming a more common term as educators better understand how literacy goes beyond written text to include other ways to look at language. For example, Warschauer (2003) and other authors discuss the importance of information literacy and multimedia literacy. Warschauer even describes what he calls computer-mediated communication literacy, which is "the ability to create, manage, and participate in effective online communication in a variety of genres and formats" (p. 2).

McCorduck (1994) notes that "we have not had much choice until now because text, whether the best representation for certain purposes or not, has dominated our intellectual lives until now. The computer is changing this.... In the computer, we have fashioned for ourselves a means of taking advantage of *all* our biological capacities to learn and to know, and to seek and find new knowledge; and this is—someday—how we *will* know" (p. 259; italics added). Murray (2000) adds that "literacy in an electronic medium is not tied to text; it may include images, sounds, and actions. Multimedia is just that" (p. 52). Although linguistic (generally textual) aspects of language are still the most common (and arguably the most important), other literacies being considered in CALL classrooms include visual and multicultural literacies. Using the World Wide Web and other electronic tools successfully for language learning requires learners to be aware of and have some skills in all of these literacies. For example, to keep the visual aspects of Web pages and other electronic texts in perspective, learners must understand how "writing in multimedia co-opts the visual as part of the text" (Murray, 2000, p. 52).

In this chapter's opening scenario, both Dari and Stephen were having trouble decoding the visual elements on their computer screen. They did not know how to "read" visual texts like these and were overwhelmed by the effort. CALL instructors can teach their learners skills in visual and other literacies to help them use electronic technologies for language learning. Ms. Johnston can find information and teaching tips at *21st Century Literacies: Tools for Reading the World* (Abilock, 1999), part of the *NoodleTools* site (www.noodletools.com/). The site presents resources and ideas for language, visual, and cultural literacies and for other literacies such as historical, information, media, political, scientific, and mathematical. Figure 9.1 shows some of these tools.

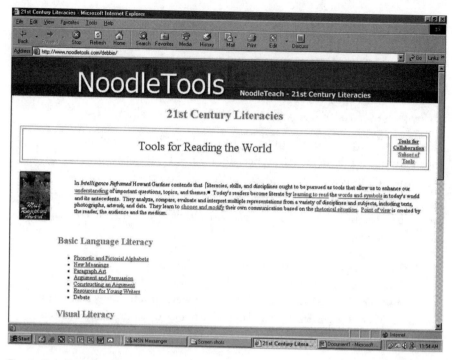

Figure 9.1. Sample page from the *NoodleTools* site.

▶ Meeting the Needs of Differently Abled Students

Some students face other special challenges in CALL environments. Not only does students' need to develop the necessary language and literacies create barriers to computer use, but other challenges, both physical and cognitive, can also make completing tasks requiring technology use very difficult for some students. Many times these challenges are not apparent until the student becomes involved in the task, as was the case with Jana and Alice in the chapter's opening scenario. To meet the needs of these and other students in CALL classrooms, teachers can apply principles of *universal design* (UD) as they develop tasks and activities.

As I noted in *CALL-EJ* (Egbert, 2004), UD is a concept that has only recently been applied to language learning. In education, materials and environments designed with UD principles in mind

- can be used by diverse learners
- provide choices for learners

- are not unnecessarily complex
- work in settings with a range of characteristics
- are easy for learners to navigate and understand
- do not depend on physical abilities to use
- accommodate physical, social, and psychological differences (adapted from Bowe, 2000; Burgstahler, 2002; Connell, et al., 1997)

Although UD works for all students, Burgstahler (2002) notes that nontraditional students benefit especially from UD: those who have physical or learning disabilities; international students; and other students with varying cultures, abilities, backgrounds, and learning needs. These students benefit because instructional materials and activities designed according to UD principles make

> the learning goals achievable by individuals with wide differences in their abilities to see, hear, speak, move, read, write, understand English, attend, organize, engage, and remember. Universal design for learning is achieved by means of flexible curricular materials and activities that provide alternatives for students with differing abilities. (Council for Exceptional Children, 1998, p. 2)

> Educators can use UD principles in their materials and environments to present information in multiple ways . . . offer multiple ways for students to interact with and respond to curricula and materials (give them choices of pace, how to respond, how to get the information) . . . [and] provide multiple ways for students to find meaning in the material and thus motivate themselves. (Bowe, 2000, p. 4)

More specifically, Strehorn (2001; see also Egbert, 2004) suggests that teachers can

- record classroom lectures and interactions not only for extra listening practice but also to provide review for students whose listening skills need additional support
- have a variety of electronic and nonelectronic resources, including dictionaries, available to learners
- have the syllabus and other course documents available in many formats, including paper, electronic, and oversized
- use books on tape, CD, or DVD
- provide students with notes from classes
- read documents out loud

- supply time frames and clear rubrics for assignments
- allow students to choose how to respond to assignments

In ESL classrooms both analog (video/audio) and digital (computer) technologies help teachers to use the principles by incorporating cueing, organizers, multimodal instruction and modeling, as well as supporting interaction. Technology can present texts in alternative modes (visually, graphically, auditorily) to meet the learning needs of the students. Whichever tools are used, they should not only assist learners in meeting objectives but also allow all learners to participate as fully as they need or want to in the process.

An important barrier to implementing UD principles in ESL classrooms is the potential conflicting and complex needs of learners from many different cultural backgrounds, with widely varying values and learning styles. Meeting these special demands poses special issues for language teachers who plan to implement principles that give everyone access to instruction. This issue is discussed later in this chapter.

▶ Computer Use in Limited Technology Contexts

Although many of the newer features of technology (e.g., real-time audio, active graphics, many-to-many communication) are useful, they are not always used to best advantage in classrooms. Reports abound in the literature of activities during which students and technology did not perform as expected. In other words, even advanced technologies can be used poorly for language and content learning. On the other hand, even with limited technology, teachers who base tasks on principles of effective language learning can provide learners with rich experiences.

Many scenarios and activities in this book have presented limited technology contexts. These contexts have limited access to technology, lack of or limited Internet access, dated software that does not match current theory, mandated use of specific technologies, or lack of hardware. It is difficult to find literature that outlines the benefits of limited technology contexts; to some educators, *benefits* and *limited* present an oxymoron. However, educators in limited technology environments find that students can more easily learn how the available technology functions, use learning strategies supported by simple technologies, do not have to deal with unnecessary and distracting audio and graphics components, focus on the learning rather than the technology, and have opportunities to use off-line resources. Despite the fact that some educators might view limited technology as a barrier to effective instruction, limited technology used in a principled way can support the development of effective language learning environments.

Much is written in the literature about barriers to using technology in classrooms; interestingly, the most common barriers are not caused by lack of technology, but by administrative, curricular, and personal needs. Barriers often include what educators see as the extra time it takes to use technology, the lack of curricular freedom, and large class sizes that make it difficult to give all students equitable access. These three aspects of technology use are discussed briefly below (teacher development in technology is discussed in chapter 10).

Time

The activities described throughout this book should not be seen as additions to an existing curriculum. Teachers can use the conditions for language learning to rethink the opportunities that they provide for learners. Because the conditions can make learning more effective and more efficient, computer-enhanced language tasks like those described in the examples can replace others that do not provide these opportunities. Teachers do not develop such activities to use exclusively, but rather to use appropriately when they meet classroom goals.

Standardized Curriculum

The use of technology should not change the goals of the curriculum. Used as a tool, technology can help teachers to meet curriculum goals more effectively and efficiently. Textbook pages and other required curriculum materials can be integrated with the technology in creative ways to give students more opportunities to learn and practice curriculum objectives.

Large Classes

Many of the activities described in this book can be adapted even for large groups of students in one-computer classrooms. For example, during a grammar exercise while the teacher or other person reads sentences from the screen, students in the class can take the role of "A" or "B" to write down odd- or even-numbered sentences. The teacher can randomly call on students to discuss answers or create groups that provide group answers. Learners then pair up to write the story. Such adaptations are especially useful in more teacher-fronted classes.

▶ The Impact of Culture

Valid barriers to using technology in classrooms do exist, however, and they range from the contextual (e.g., 200 people with one laptop) to the administrative (e.g., lack of funding, lack of knowledge support), from the legal (e.g., obtaining parental permission for student technology use) to the physical (e.g., migraine headaches resulting from screen blinking). Because teachers can easily observe these barriers, they can more easily acknowledge and deal with them. Other barriers, however, are not so obvious, and they also can impact student achievement in CALL classrooms. The most pervasive of these less obvious barriers is culture.

Culture can have an impact in CALL classrooms in many ways, some of them similar to its impact in nontechnology classrooms and others a factor of the tool. For example, student learning styles on and around computers can be different for learners from different backgrounds, and learners may use different strategies for the same task (e.g., writing) when they use a different tool. In addition, culture may influence how people perceive the computer (Warshauer, 1998, 1999). As in this chapter's opening scenario, these influences can be misunderstood. Culture also has an impact on what students learn. Whose culture and language are portrayed by the electronic tools that learners use, and how the culture and language are portrayed, can influence how much and what learners understand and also how they feel about the work they are doing.

How can teachers be more aware of culture's impact in CALL classrooms? They can do the same kinds of things they would do in any classroom, but in CALL classrooms technology can help. For example, teachers can value learners' first languages by offering them plenty of first language support by using native language Web sites and software, bilingual electronic storybooks, and translation services such as *BabelFish* (http://www.babelfish.com/). Teachers can develop greater cultural sensitivity themselves by studying and communicating with members of other cultures. Software and Internet resources can help them to see cultures through different eyes (both emic and etic views) and to study culture deeply. A starting point for teachers and learners might be the country reports offered by *CultureGrams* (http://www.culturegrams.com/). In addition, teachers can work with learners to develop new literacies and strategies that will help them be successful in CALL classrooms.

▶ Legal Issues

With access to the Internet, ever-expanding resources on the World Wide Web, and the profusion of software programs across the world come legal responsibilities for teachers, students, and technology administrators. U.S. law addresses three main areas of concern:

1. student safe use
2. potential for plagiarism
3. fair use

Safe Use

Learners using technology face a variety of risks, particularly on the World Wide Web. The Online Safety Project (2002) notes that

> Statistically, probably the greatest risk is that a child will . . . encounter people in chat areas and newsgroups who are mean or obnoxious. Another "risk" is that a child will spend a lot of wasted time in areas that aren't all that productive.

Exposure to inappropriate material, harassment, lack of privacy, and even legal and financial problems can result from using the Internet. Many schools and language programs already have policies in place to avoid such problems. The first step to avoiding these problems is to make sure that learners using computers are supervised. Classes should establish rules for online safety like those at *SafeKids.Com* (*Rules for Online Safety,* www.safekids.com/; see Figure 9.2), and the consequences of not following the rules should be clear. Teachers can adapt the *Kids' Pledge* (see *Family Contract for Online Safety,* www.safekids.com/) for their classes, and they can discuss it with students. (In language classrooms, instructors might want to add visual elements and provide translated versions to make the pledge easier to understand.) Many schools have posted their rules; see, for example, the rules posted by the Roman Catholic Diocese of Albany (RCDA), New York, in the United States (RCDA, n.d.). The online magazine *Teaching Today* publishes an informational guide on safe use called *Internet Safety and Security: What Teachers Need to Know* (Glencoe/McGraw-Hill, 2004). These and other resources can keep teachers and students out of trouble.

Plagiarism

In the United States and many other places, the term *plagiarism* means to use something that another person has created or owns and claim it as one's own

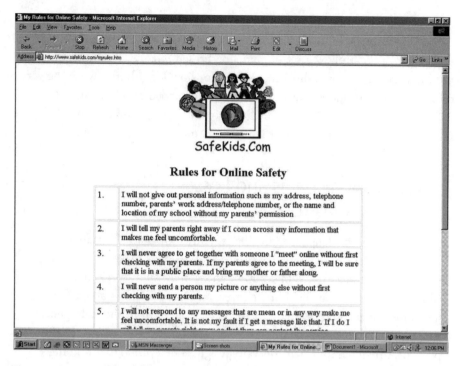

Figure 9.2. Some of the rules from SafeKids.com.

work. Plagiarism is against the law in the United States, and most schools have policies to deal with it; however, plagiarism is a cultural artifact and learners from cultures where writing and other published works are publicly owned (in other words, anyone may use them and not have to attribute them to the original author) may not easily understand the concept. Therefore, policies for dealing with electronic plagiarism in language classrooms must take into consideration the learner's belief systems.

With all the materials on the Web and special sites where learners can go to download prewritten essays, plagiarism in schools seems to be increasing. Harris (2002) provides clear steps to teachers for avoiding plagiarism and addressing the issue in classrooms before it happens. However, if plagiarism does occur, the *Dead Giveaways* page (http://www.plagiarized.com/) suggests how to spot it. If you suspect that all or part of a students' essay may be plagiarized, you can check it using the free *Internet Essay Exposer* (Clare, 2000).

Fair Use

Copyright law in the United States gives authors or creators ownership of what they create; this includes graphics, text, and video. Violating copyright, or using materials that someone else owns, can be very costly if the owner sues the violator in court. Teachers can use copyrighted materials for their instruction if they follow a set of guidelines called *fair use*. These guidelines outline what can be used, how much, and for how long, but they can be very difficult to understand. A clear explanation is provided by University of Maryland's University College (2004). To be safe, teachers should use materials marked *copyright-free* or contact the owner for permission.

▶ Conclusion: Gains and Losses in CALL Classrooms

Using technology for language learning is neither a panacea nor an antidote. There are gains and losses in every choice that teachers make (Bowers, 1998; Burniske & Monke, 2001; Jung, 2003), and while educators think about CALL's benefits for language learners, they also need to think about the opportunities that using technology might take away from them. In general, Bowers (1998) notes that computers inherently amplify or reduce certain aspects of experience and that software designers determine the thinking patterns used in the software that they develop. He advocates that both teachers and students study these phenomena. More specifically, a teacher's choice to use, for example, voice chatting over the Internet to help students practice listening and speaking also means learners participate in oral activity devoid of the pragmatic examples that they need to develop effective language skills. Although it is not always possible to foresee what incidental gains and losses teachers and students will experience from using technology, teachers should view technology in language teaching and learning with critical vigilance. In fact, if they take a careful look at how they might best prepare language learners for their futures, they might discover that learners do not need to use or know technology. Saying that all learners must have certain technology skills ignores the fact that people live their lives in many different ways.

▶ Teachers' Voices

I would like to present two scenarios that occur frequently in my job. Scenario 1: A third-grade boy has horrendous handwriting—it is big and has incorrect size (capitals and small letters look the same), has little or no spacing and spelling is terrible—invented at best. He hates writing stories or anything because it is so labor intensive. His handwriting is starting to interfere with his school work and he has great ideas but refuses to write because it is so challenging. Learning to keyboard is presented as an option but then the question of do we abandon handwriting altogether always comes up. The quandary, do we use the technology or is it a crutch? Scenario 2: A student is proficiently using an Alphasmart (a word processing device). The student is a terrible speller. For reports he is allowed to use spell check. He uses it on a regular basis but he is still taking spelling tests to learn to spell. It is [standardized testing] time. The student is allowed to word process on his computer but not spell check because it would allow the student an unfair advantage because no one else can spell check any words. The story has to be scribed into the booklet by someone else. All students can use a dictionary to correct or check spelling. Does the technology give an unfair advantage? Should the technology be an option for all students? Does the technology rob the students of the opportunity to learn to spell?

Audiotapes/CDs are great to use for listening and vocabulary skills. Our science and social studies texts have the chapters on tape so that struggling readers can understand what's going on. In order to enhance the tape's value, my teaching partner and I use it in collaboration with the book and with any visuals provided (posters, overhead images). By reading along, listening, and seeing what the chapter is about, the students are provided with a strong visual of what's being said on the tape.

There is so much information out there that it sometimes becomes a hassle to use the Web. Furthermore, I noticed that there is a lot of outdated info online. I was trying to find information on out of state school districts and found that some sites have not been updated since 1998! So besides checking to see if the site is still up, check the date when it was made. I'd rather find no info than outdated info.

Computer use does take some time, especially when first getting started. I agree that 'baby steps' are needed when first starting out. This can even be in your creating documents on the computer just to get yourself familiar with using it. There are so many things that can be done on the computer that it can be overwhelming if you try to take them all on. It might be good to pick just one program that you could use. Get really familiar with it yourself; then gradually create a lesson that will allow your students to become involved with it too. You can start out teaching a small group of students how to do whatever activity you want them to try out, and let them teach others in the class. Maybe set a goal for yourself of creating documents for your students to use this year, and then next year creating one or two lessons that will involve your students actually using the computer. You do want the use on the computer to be effective and efficient, so don't feel that you have to use it all the time. For right now, you might be more efficient and effective in many lessons without it. (But don't let that stop you from learning how to use the computer.) The other thing is you don't want to use the computer to the exclusion of other activities that are better suited for a particular learning objective. . . . For example, if I wanted to take my students on a virtual field trip to a place they would not otherwise be able to go to, then the computer is a good vehicle for that. Where I think computers can be overused is when they are used for illustrating or teaching things that could be better done without them. We learn through our senses, and the more senses we can involve in a student's learning the better. The computer just doesn't involve as many senses as we can when we allow students to smell touch, taste, etc. The other thing is we learn best when we touch with both hands (and utilize both sides of the brain), and the computer leaves some of that out. Also computers can limit creativity. They can also enhance creativity—depending on the activity. So you need to pick activities carefully.

We have used Word, PowerPoint, Publisher, and Excel this year, almost exclusively. The Usborne software (First [Thousand] Words) is pretty cheap, and my kids (past years) have really enjoyed it. I used that this year with a monolingual student I had. He used that as a guide and made a Spanish-English dictionary to 'help me learn my Spanish.' The other software I have used for remediation and for enrichment. I also have had a computer schedule for kids. They are required to do "x" number of activities on a particular piece of software. I have a time when the rest of the class is doing independent work and the assigned students may use the computers, or they may use them during any free time periods they have. Many kids also like coming in the room early to use the computers. Last year I had an after school time when kids could stay to do homework and use the computers when they were finished. Other than that, I have a math review time when 1/3 of the class is on the computers doing specific math lessons with worksheets (or external documents) to guide them, another group is working with me, and another group is working with a parapro.— I agree, I don't like to just 'plug them in,' but for those free time periods, and periods before school starts, I have let them explore some of the software, and I think it has been OK.

We also have a standard form that goes home at the beginning of the year. If students don't bring it back then they can't use the Internet. The permission form also serves as an agreement to use technology appropriately. I haven't had any parents not allow their child to use the Internet at school. Our district also has many sites blocked. Sometimes sites that shouldn't be blocked are, which is a bit frustrating, but MUCH BETTER than the alternative of having nothing blocked. Even when we think we're being safe something will show up, students will giggle, and I'll rush over to find an exposed belly button. OH MY :-). Anymore you can't go online without having something questionable pop-up. We just have to educate our students about what is acceptable and appropriate and help them become mature and responsible individuals.

There are a lot of potential barriers when it comes to using and having computers in the classroom setting. I think that by starting with those barriers that can be changed is a good beginning point. For example, we can't change that all of our students don't have equal opportunities and experience with computers before they come to us, but we can change our current level of knowledge and training in computer skills, etc. This can also be done relatively inexpensively. Most of us know quite a few computer savvy people who would be willing to meet with us once a week to work on some skills, etc. Also, a lot of it is just taking the time to "mess around" on the computer and become familiar with different software programs. At least for me, once I feel comfortable with something, then I'm more willing to try and search out ways to implement and practice my knowledge and skills. I see quite a few barriers, and yes, they can be frustrating, but I also see ways that some of these can be broken down.

I agree that time is a key factor in computer skills and work. Also not everyone will bring the same level of prior knowledge or skills with them to the classroom. This is especially true in [my school district], where many students come from low-income families. As teachers, what can we do to ensure that everyone has "equal access" to computers? We can't necessarily change the home environment or situation, but we can make accommodations at school or within the curriculum. It is important to ensure that all students get their turn at the computer. Timers, assigned roles or tasks can help with this. Also, for those students who naturally need more exposure, giving free-time during lunch to work on the computer or maybe before or after school can be one way to help "boost" those students. I know quite a few schools are beginning to have computer labs that are open before and after school, and also during lunch for students to stay and work on their assignments, etc. I think that is a great idea.

I have taken my adult ESL students to the public library in the past to show them the free computers available to them. Once I have taught them how to use the Internet in my classroom, I show them how to access it using the public library computers. We practice getting onto www.nwlincs.org page so that they know how to access it when the college is not in session or when they are not able to attend classes anymore. Hopefully they will feel comfortable accessing the many resources I have shown them on the Web, like Mapquest and others, but if they access nothing other than the NWlincs one I will feel like I have accomplished a lot. This Web site has so many links (ESL cafes, ESL exercises, maps) that they can practice and grow their English without me.

chapter*10*

▶ Teacher Development

▶ Focus

In this chapter you will

- discover professional development opportunities in CALL

- learn about resources and tools for teachers in CALL classrooms

- reflect on the importance of teacher inquiry to CALL practice

R ead the following scenario and think about the barriers that Ms. Plenner faced in implementing a CALL activity.

Ms. Plenner's supervisor was pushing her to use the new computer lab in her school. He assigned her a time slot in the lab in the middle of the week and strongly recommended that she have her students use some of the ESL software that the school had recently purchased. Ms. Plenner was not familiar with any of the software packages and had little experience with the Internet other than using a basic e-mail program. Her curriculum, already packed, did not include ideas for using technology, and she had not had any training in using technology during her teacher certification classes. She did not have time before the middle of the week to investigate the lab or the software or even to talk to her colleagues about using technology with second language students.

Ms. Plenner's students, most of whom did not have other access to computers in the economically poor neighborhood in which they lived, were excited (and nervous) about using computers in class and expressed their hope that their language learning would increase as a result. Ms. Plenner decided to take her students to the lab and let them choose what they wanted to do, hoping that they would catch on to the software fairly quickly because they were highly motivated.

The class time in the computer lab was a disaster. Ms. Plenner did not know that someone would need to turn the computers on and each student would need a password to log on. She expected that there would be a lab monitor, but there was not one. After she had spent time helping students access the computers, the students did not know which program to choose. Ms. Plenner picked one from the desktop that helped students practice grammar and asked everyone to do unit one. Two students said that grammar drills were not useful for them and that they wanted to talk to native English speakers online. After several other students seemed confused about how to answer some of the questions in the grammar unit because it used idiomatic language and contexts that they did not understand, Ms. Plenner told the students to return to the classroom, promising that she would figure out how to use the lab better for future sessions.

▶ Overview of CALL Professional Development Opportunities

Pressure from the school administration to use technology contributed to Ms. Plenner's problems using CALL. Because she was not given a chance to learn about the technology and its uses beforehand, she was not prepared to use the lab, she did not consider using the computers as tools to help meet her goals, and she did not set up tasks that met optimal language learning conditions. This scenario is an exaggeration, but many teachers meet at least some of the same barriers to effective use of CALL: lack of time, training, freely accessible resources, and incentive. These barriers are often difficult to overcome, but many resources and tools exist to help teachers and administrators understand these barriers and to surmount them. This chapter outlines ways for teachers to get started in creating plans for professional development in CALL and to begin to develop strategies for CALL that fit the needs of their classrooms and contexts.

▶ Getting Started: Planning for Professional Development

Ms. Plenner realizes that the her students' success is closely linked to her knowledge and practice as a teacher (Diaz-Maggioli, 2003) and that she needs to acquire the knowledge and skills necessary to use the technology in the lab effectively; in other words, Ms. Plenner needs to engage in professional development (PD) on the use of technology in language teaching and learning. As a relatively new teacher, however, Ms. Plenner is not sure where to start; the area of CALL seems overwhelmingly large and new to her, and she feels that she must learn as much as she can as quickly as possible.

Diaz-Maggioli (2003) notes that the purpose of professional development is "to promote effective teaching that results in learning gains for all students" (p. 2). Many print and electronic resources are dedicated to this goal. Among the best is the North Central Regional Educational Laboratory's (NCREL) thorough and theoretically sound Web site (Learning Point Associates, 2004b), which can help teachers plan and carry out professional development activities. Part of this site features a toolkit to help programs and schools design professional development programs. This resource provides step-by-step guidelines for the development process with handouts and other support materials. NCREL's *Using Technology in PD* site (Learning Point Associates, 2004d) provides additional resources and ideas about both using technology for PD and studying technology as PD. NCREL's *Technology Professional Development* site (Learning Point Associates, 2004c) has resources that can help teachers detail their vision for using technology and then find out how best to make it happen.

Perhaps the most useful part of the NCREL site is the *Learning with Technology Profile Tool* (Learning Point Associates, 2004a; see Figure 10.1). This survey helps teachers to review the characteristics of engaged learning and technology use and to reflect on how they and their class, program, or school is prepared to engage students in learning, with and without using technology, regardless of language or content area. Other sets of guidelines for professional development and surveys to help get started exist both on the Web and in hard copy from government and private organizations.

Once you have decided what you want or need to know, you can explore the resources available to help teachers find out about CALL.

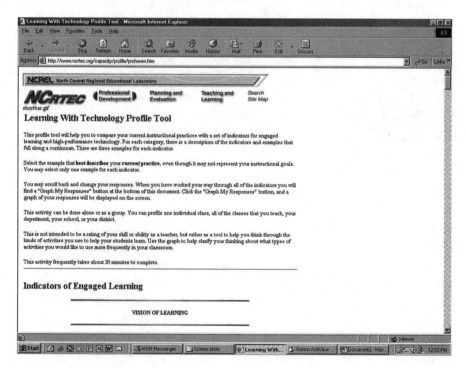

Figure 10.1. Part of NCREL's *Learning with Technology Profile Tool.*

▶ General Resources for Teacher Development

For teachers with the time and finances, many organizations offer online courses, standard face-to-face courses, conferences (online and face-to-face), or training sessions. Teachers with less time might take advantage of the many books, articles, and magazines dealing with technology; develop teacher study groups; participate in discussion lists such as TESLCA-L (City University of New York, 2004); or attend short in-service workshops. Murphey (2003) describes these and other professional development opportunities. Whichever opportunities you choose, getting the most out of these experiences is important. Chao (2003) suggests that after choosing an activity, teachers should develop a plan to help meet goals effectively. Teachers can ask, "What do I need to know immediately? What would most support my classroom goals? In what specific ways will this activity assist me?" Teaching with technology is a large and complex subject, so the activity should focus clearly on professional development. The resources in this chapter and at the end of this book provide excellent starting points for development in CALL.

Saving Time by Learning How to Use the Web

An important first step to development using Web-based resources is learning to search the Web efficiently and effectively. Verizon publishes amazing resources at the *Enlighten Me* (Verizon, 2004a) and *Super Thinkers* (Verizon, 2003) pages, which Fablevision has developed. On the *Enlighten Me* page, check out the multimedia *Peetnik Mysteries* and the *Mental Market* materials. To help get you started, this site includes an excellent tool, the *Internet Learning Tutor* (Verizon, 2004b).

Efficient Web use includes knowing the differences between browsers and how to use advanced search terms. Gray (n.d.) has posted a useful overview, and Barker (2003) provides a thorough tutorial comparing the most popular browsers (Netscape and Explorer) and search tools, and he includes handouts and definitions of jargon. A simple and useful tool to help teachers and learners conduct direct searches is *NoodleQuest* (NoodleTools, 2004). At this site, you can input your search information, and it will show you which search engine will be the best for your search. The *Yahoo!* search engine (Yahoo!, 2004) provides a list of helpful materials for Web searchers with various levels of technical knowledge. In learning to search the Web, practice does make better, if not perfect. Of course, learning takes time; until you feel more comfortable conducting Web searches, you can find plenty of books and other materials with lists of great links and other technology resources for teachers. Colleagues are also great sources for useful materials and information on using technology in language classrooms.

The time spent on learning to search well will be rewarded by access to a countless number of resources, mostly free, for use by CALL teachers. Below are listed some sample search terms followed by examples of professional resources that can be found using the *Google* search engine (http://www.google.com). The special symbols used (e.g., +, " ") in the search term box help define the exact parameters of the search. Find out more about how to use these characters in one of the overviews mentioned earlier.

"lesson plan" + ESL

Lesson plan sites abound on the Web; one popular resource is http://www.lessonplanspage.com. Other useful sites include the *Lesson Plans* page at the *Educator's Reference Desk* (formerly AskERIC; www.eduref.org/), which lists lessons by category and has a searchable database, and ESL-specific lessons at http://www.esl-lounge.com/. With the thousands of lessons on the Web, teachers can adapt the wheel rather than reinventing it, thereby saving precious time.

"computer-assisted language learning" journal

Teachers can peruse many e-journals for information on CALL, including *Teaching English with Technology* (International Association of Teachers of English as a Foreign Language, 2004) and the academic research-based *Language Learning & Technology* (http://llt.msu.edu/).

"software reviews" + ESL

This search term results in pages of well-written and accessible reviews of all kinds of language teaching software, including *CALL Software Reviews* (Duber, 2002) at the University of California, Berkeley, which provides reviews of software for a wide range of language contexts, and *Software Reviews* (Ohio University, 2004).

language listserv

Searching on this simple term finds, among other sites, the *Foreign Language Teaching Forum* (Univerity at Buffalo, 2002), which provides instructions on how to join the electronic discussion list and contains links to the archives. Narrowing this search to "ESL listserv" brings up pages such as *Useful Lists for Linguistics and English* (Kitao & Kitao, 1997).

EFL "online conference"

This search brings up entries about conferences such as the Second International Online Conference on Second and Foreign Language Teaching and Research (The Reading Matrix, 2003).

"free ESL materials" + teachers

This general search brings up everything from song lyrics, board game printouts, and lessons to dictionaries and job listings. Sites such as *Wordsurfing* (McCulloch, 2004) provide examples and interesting ideas for helping learners to acquire new vocabulary.

Learning to search efficiently can provide teachers with many focused resources to help them reach their professional development goals and overcome barriers to using technology.

Incentives: Tools for Teachers

Learning to search the Web efficiently and being able to use its abundant resources effectively can serve as one incentive for teachers to use technology tools. Release time and extra resources are also excellent (and crucial) incentives to support teacher development in CALL. However, many programs and schools cannot afford to provide these or other inducements. For some teachers, incentive grows as they learn more about computer technologies and how these technologies can (a) support learning in language classrooms, (b) help teachers use time efficiently, and (c) provide ways for teachers to do their jobs more effectively. For example, computer software such as ParentOrganizer (n.v.) and SchoolMessenger USB (n.v.) helps teachers contact parents and notify them of school events. With this software, teachers can send a voice message via the telephone to parents or students; send wake up calls to students who are often tardy; and let parents know about meetings, homework, and student progress. *Gaggle.Net* (http://www.gaggle.net/) removes the worry about what students are writing in e-mail messages by letting you access every message that students send and receive. Max's Toolbox (1.5.1) imposes a child-friendly interface on the popular Microsoft Office products, making them simpler to use and far easier to teach. In teacher MOOs like *Tapped In* (http://www.tappedin.org/), teachers can meet and work remotely with other teachers, sharing ideas, information, and empathy. The Web even has a tool called *Citation Machine* (Warlick 2004), which will help you format citations for reports and other work, and a Permission Template that teachers and students can use to request permission to use information from Web sources (Warlick, 2003). Being able to use these time-saving and community-building tools can motivate some teachers to learn and use technology.

Another possible incentive for teachers to learn more about technology and to improve their teaching is easy access to answers. Teachers whose forté is not linguistics, for example, could check the *EnglishClub.com* (http:// grammar.englishclub.com/) before class to get a quick brush up on parts of speech, check specific articles, update themselves on English language teaching terminology, or locate answers to grammar questions that they were not able to answer for their learners during class. Teachers may also check *English Grammar on the Web* (Byrd, 2001), which "was planned to give ESL/ EFL teachers background information on teaching grammar in ESL/EFL classes as well as material to use in their classes. The site includes grammatical information, course syllabi and lesson plans, and links to other sites." In addition, Purdue University's *Online Writing Lab* (Purdue University, 2004) provides resources and exercises with handouts. American University Library offers another site for linguistically challenged teachers: *Language and Linguistics: TESOL* (American University, 2004). This list contains links to numerous linguistics sites that teachers can tap for information.

Discovering other teaching tools that save time and money and can contribute to learner achievement can help motivate teachers to learn more about effective uses of technology. For example, Cohen (2003) provides an excellent overview of strategy training for language learners. Free presentation tools are another inducement for teachers. Copyright-free graphics that can be included in presentations to make teacher lessons potentially more accessible can be found at sites such as *The Amazing Picture Machine* (Learning Point Associates, 1998). *Projects by Students of English* at *Linguistic Funland* (Pfaff-Harris, n.d.) shows some of the outcomes of using technology in language learning; this site can generate excitement and provide models to scaffold the creation of such projects by other learners.

There are many ways for teachers to learn about the using technology in language teaching and learning and to use technology during the professional development process. The discovery or exploration phase will require the teacher to invest some time, but the eventual savings by having access to resources, information, models, and a community of learners in similar contexts can make the initial outlay well worth it.

▶ Critical Inquiry in CALL

Many educators are critical of technology use in education, for good reasons (see, e.g., critiques by Cuban, 2001; Oppenheimer, 1997; Postman, 1993). In short, these authors argue that technology has not changed education for the better and that billions of dollars that might be spent in other ways are being wasted on technology that is not used well. The criticism that technology will not improve education is valid; however, the effective use of technology could improve opportunities for learners, and that is up to the teachers who design the instruction. This chapter has thus far described teacher professional development activities that can help teachers become more effective users of technology in their teaching and in their own learning. Teacher inquiry is another activity worth examining because it can impact both teacher professional development and effective classroom technology use.

The preface of this book notes that its emphasis is practical, and nothing enhances practice like inquiry. Teachers have their own ways of teaching well, but the literature presents a consensus that reflecting on and investigating one's teaching can improve it. Dana and Silva (2003) note that teacher inquiry can help teachers "untangle some of the complexity of teaching that occurs within their four walls, raise teachers' voices in discussions of educational reform, and ultimately, transform assumptions about the teaching profession itself" (p. 2). Teachers perform informal inquiry daily, but more formal inquiry projects can lead teachers and their inquiry partners to focus more specifically on a question or problem. Generally, the steps of an inquiry project include

- thinking about something in your classroom that you would like to understand better or know more about
- deciding how you might go about answering the question
- gathering the data you need to answer it, and figuring out what answer the data you collected gives you
- deciding what to do next (what action to take)
- sharing your experience or even trying a new technique or idea

Often, the words *I wonder* generate a useful question to explore (much as they do for student inquiry projects, as described in chapter 6).

In CALL classrooms, an inquiry project plan might look something like this:

► **Question:** I wonder what my English learners talk about when they are around the computer. How on task are they? I'd like to discover how effective/efficient the tasks that we use regularly are in this regard.

How to answer: I need to get samples of their talk and try to figure out how these relate to the task and other variables. First, I need to read about tasks and see how other people have gathered this kind of information.

Data gathering: I need to videotape or tape-record conversations to get an idea of the interaction and its content (keeping in mind that this might make them speak differently than they otherwise would). Perhaps I can also get them to reflect on how much time they spend on task, what else they do while they are at the computer, and why.

Analyzing the data: I will compare the record of the conversations to students' perceptions of what is going on and what my goals are. I will double-check my results with them and perhaps initiate a conversation about what I found.

Follow up: If there does not seem to be a problem, I will continue to construct tasks the way I have been. If there is a problem, I would like to experiment with other ways to construct tasks to help students focus better and stay on task. I will share my results with my teacher group and ask for suggestions.

Teachers can ask and directly investigate an infinite number of important questions in the context of the classroom. Inquiry can be conducted with other teachers, in conjunction with the administration, and even with students as inquiry partners. Teachers who inquire about their technology practice provide role models for students to question their learning and reflect on how they might improve.

► Conclusion

This chapter has discussed professional development opportunities in CALL, presented resources and tools for teachers, and noted the importance of teacher inquiry to CALL practice. Although taking advantage of some of these opportunities can assist Ms. Plenner (in the opening scenario) in meeting her language students' needs more effectively, she still has other barriers to overcome. Most important, she needs to help her supervisor and perhaps others at her school to understand that effective CALL use is not the result of being assigned a time in the computer lab and using the available software; rather, it comes from understanding principles for language learning and technology use, careful planning, and critical inquiry into the process and outcomes of computer-enhanced tasks.

► Teachers' Voices

I have made use of ABC Teach as a teacher resource of free stuff. It covers topics like reading comprehension, shape books, theme units, reports, fun activities. It also appears that there are many more tips for $25 a year. It had a special ESL category. The link is www.abcteach.com.

There is a need of an ongoing staff development for teachers to implement and become more knowledgeable in technology. We all need to know how to research and evaluate the accuracy, relevance, appropriateness, comprehensiveness of electronic information resources to be used by students. Creating a learning community between teachers can really empower individual professional growth.

I love the computer, don't get me wrong, they've got all those fancy buttons and things :-) It's just that there are so many NEW and exciting options for using technology, I just don't know where to begin! I'd be willing to put the time into trying something out if someone, could TELL me which ONE is the best for me to start out with. I know, I know, there isn't one 'best' program or Web site, just like there isn't one 'best' teaching technique. But I need a place to begin that fits in with my learners (fifth grade, many ELL), my curriculum (EALRs!!! [Washington State's Essential Academic Learning Requirements]), my philosophy (everyone should have the opportunity to learn in the style/environment most suitable to them), and my time (limited). Also, I want the program I try out to be interactive, so the students like it, and effective and efficient, so my administration approves it. What do you say? Do you have a recommendation for me?

I have always had the problem of time limitations in the past, and I guess that it is always going to be a problem. However, this year I feel as though I have a better handle on it. I am approaching it a little differently. I just decide what learning or project I want the kids to accomplish. Then [I] figure out what skills they will need to accomplish that, and I give mini-lessons until they have enough background to accomplish the task. The guiding rule in the room is "Ask three, then me." So students always ask three other students how to do things on the computer before they ask me. They end up learning a lot from each other this way. I let them in the room before school starts, and they get their computer skills nailed down during this time, too. We just started a bulletin board with tech tips, and they check that out for cool things to try out on technology tools. While this seems really simple and like a 'no brainer' I just wasn't using my time very well with technology until this year. Technology training for me has made a big difference in my efficiency in using technology with my kids.

chapter *11*

▶ Conclusion: My Favorite CALL Things

▶ **Focus**

In this chapter you will consider "bests" in the field of CALL.

As you read the following scenario, reflect on what message you will take away from this book.

Dr. Egbert is sitting at her desk typing the concluding chapter for her teacher resource book called *CALL Essentials*. She has provided an overview of the major issues in technology use and supplied teachers with resources but feels there is something missing. What does she want to say as an endnote? What message does she want teachers to take away from this book? As she agonizes over the decision, she reflects on the successes and failures of her ESL and EFL students in CALL lessons, thinks about how much she has learned while writing the book, and ponders how much technology has changed in the years she has been a teacher. She reviews the criticisms of technology use and hopes that teachers will become—and show their students how to become—critical consumers and users. She decides to end the book with her experiences in CALL classrooms with CALL technologies, hoping that they will serve as a discussion point for further exploration into the field of CALL.

▶ Overview

I could say much more about CALL than I have said in this book—there are many more resources, ideas, and technologies to discuss—but it does cover what I consider to be the essentials. Because it is fairly brief, much of this book has been relatively generic, presenting basic suggestions and ideas. Some of the ideas presented I use in class, and some I do not (or have not yet). In this chapter I go beyond a simple "what's out there" to discuss some of the ideas and technologies that work for my students and me. The format of this chapter is much like a "best of" list, with the top three in each category explained. Teachers can reflect on their own knowledge and experience by making a similar list.

▶ Three Favorite Software Programs or Companies

Good software made for English language learners does exist, but most of this targeted software does not fit with my teaching style or my language classes' communicative goals. My three favorite software programs or companies are therefore commercial publishers of educational software developed in general for native speakers.

1. **Tom Snyder Productions**

   I have mentioned Tom Snyder Productions (TSP) products many times throughout this book. I started with the TSP software packages National Inspirer (Version 1.0) and Decisions, Decisions: The Environment (Version 2.0), and I still find them useful and effective. Newer products such as Neighborhood Map Machine (Version 2.0) have kept the earlier software's simple, high-quality, principled approach. A crucial component is the teacher's guides—they are thorough, multidisciplinary, pedagogically sound, and they usually mention techniques for using the software successfully to achieve language and content goals with English language learners.

2. **Edmark**

   Edmark, now part of Riverdeep, provides open-ended, content-based software. From the House series that includes science, literacy, and other programs, to the Thinkin' Things collections (Version 3.1) and Imagination Express (Version 1.1) series mentioned previously, this software contains scaffolding for English language learners and enough open-ended opportunities that all students can work to their ability. Many of the software packages are mapped to the standards in the content areas. Like TSP, Edmark provides thorough and useful teacher's guides, allowing teachers and students to jump right in.

3. **Usborne**

   My students love using Usborne's Animated First Thousand Words (n.v.). The many simple and fun multimodal vocabulary games captivate students. (Usborne's also has an amazing teaching tool in the Puzzle series of texts, and they produce other useful software packages.)

▶ Three Most Useful Hardware Devices

Of course there is no CALL without the computer, which technically means the central processing unit (CPU). Taking for granted that the CPU, monitor, and keyboard are vital components, in my opinion CALL classrooms must have at least three other devices.

1. **USB Memory Key**

   This tiny device, about 3 inches long and 1 inch wide, provides accessible, nearly indestructible storage for your files that you can wear around your neck on a lanyard, clip onto your key chain, or put in your pocket (where a floppy disk might look strange). USB keys do not require any special software to run, and they can be used on Macs and PCs interchangeably. To me, this is the best hardware and memory advance in years. (See Figure 11.1.)

2. **Digital Camera**

   Aside from taking still shots that teachers or students can download and use instantly, many digital cameras can also record short videos. Digital pictures are ready to be sent by e-mail, posted easily to Web pages, or integrated into presentations. The use of digital cameras can support authentic student-centered activities such as creating presentations about their families and neighborhoods, recording scientific information, and introducing themselves to keypals across the world.

Figure 11.1. USB Memory Key by DELL Computers.

3. **Color Printer**

This is not new technology, but it has more recently begun to create some new opportunities for teachers and learners. Aside from printing photos, color printers can produce colorful t-shirt iron-ons, posters, newsletters, calendars, pamphlets, and a range of other student products. Color printers can be purchased for approximately US$50 as of this writing, so if you use the ink carefully, they are a bargain.

▶ Three Most Used Web Sites

I wanted to list my favorite Web sites here, but there are many from which to choose. The three below are those that I use most often as part of my professional life.

1. **Teachers of English to Speakers of Other Languages, Inc. (TESOL)**

This site (http://www.tesol.org/) has links to the CALL Interest Section; information about meetings, conferences, and policy issues; descriptions of new publications; and a host of other features to keep educators connected to the profession.

2. **Educational Resources Information Center (ERIC)**

Throughout this book, ERIC Digests are listed as resources for exploring almost every CALL-related topic. The ERIC resources provide basic information on almost any educational topic and references for deeper exploration. Sites for the database, clearinghouses, and other resources are currently moving because funding has changed, so the U.S. Department of Education suggests that, rather than looking at individual clearinghouses, users check the main government site (http://www.eric.ed.gov/) to find what they need.

3. **Google**

Although Web search engines have proliferated on the Internet and educators have different preferences, I still find *Google* (http://www.google.com/) the easiest to use. Few ads, no pop-up windows, and an outstanding hit rate make *Google* a site I use almost every day for both work and personal Web searching.

▶ Three Favorite CALL Activities

In general my favorite CALL activities are those that most motivate my students while helping them reach their content and language objectives. I have mentioned many such activities already, but three in particular include WebQuests (http://webquest.sdsu.edu), action mazes, and making things.

1. **WebQuests**

   A well-developed WebQuest supports the conditions for optimal language learning environments in many ways. It supports students as they work toward content and language objectives, provides them with a kind of structured autonomy and authentic tasks, offers them opportunities to interact with teammates and others, and exposes them to many different kinds of language and ways to produce it. Because the outline is the same for all WebQuests, students know what to expect after the first one. Though currently not many WebQuests are directed specifically toward ESL learners, more are posted regularly, and they are worth checking from time to time.

2. **Action Mazes**

   There is nothing like creating an action maze to help students think about the consequences of certain actions, understand that any decision can have multiple consequences, and use lots of creative language. When developing action mazes, students can use focused language and any number of technologies, including voice, text, and graphics. Action mazes can also function as assessment tools, providing information on how learners understood the content of a lesson (this works especially well with action mazes dealing with cultural concepts).

3. **Making Things**

   When students create with technology, whether they generate an action maze, graphic organizer, WebQuest, bumper sticker, or newsletter, the convenience with which language can be entered (typed), checked, shared, and revised takes the focus off of technology and keeps the activity focused on language and content objectives and using language in different ways. And there is nothing like the excitement generated by learners making something that they are invested in.

▶ Three Best Electronic Resources for CALL Teachers

Again, it is a hard choice, because there are so many options. However, the following three resources have multiple uses and help make both teaching and learning more effective and efficient.

1. **E-mail**

   I do not know any teachers without e-mail capabilities, but I do know many teachers who do not take advantage of all the capabilities. An e-mail account enables teachers to join electronic discussion groups, build relationships with students and families, contact experts around the world, receive daily news reports, and more. Teachers who use technology for language learning should use their e-mail to join relevant professional electronic discussion lists, which can be the best electronic resource available by e-mail.

2. **Presentation Software**

   HyperStudio (Version 3.0) and Microsoft PowerPoint have a gentle learning curve and similar capabilities. Both software packages allow teachers to spice up their lectures with animation, voice, text, and graphics; create interactive texts such as action mazes; and provide students with platforms from which to create all kinds of language-based products. Along with a word processor, this is software that every classroom should have and use.

3. **Web Page Publishing Software**

   Many software packages are available that can create Web pages, from the ubiquitous FrontPage to all kinds of packages developed for use specifically with young learners. I have already explored numerous activities that involve creating, using, and sharing Web pages. It is important for learners using Web resources to understand that the Web is not magic, that it is accessible to them, and that they can control their own small corner of this vast resource. By making even simple and effective Web pages, learners can come to know the power of language and technology.

▶ Three Best Commercial Web Sites

Many educators tend to avoid commercial Web sites for a variety of reasons, but these sites can serve as effective resources for traditional language learning activities, making the learning more efficient and authentic.

1. **Travel Sites**

   A common activity in language and content classes is for students to plan a trip somewhere, including estimating expenses. They used to estimate travel expenses from ads or other sources, but now they can get exact flight, hotel, and rental car information from travel sites on the Web such as *Travelocity* (http://www.travelocity.com/) and *Expedia* (http://www.expedia.com/).

2. **Store Sites**

   Amazon (http://www.amazon.com/) and sites like it are great not only for ordering things, but also for culture-based activities. For example, you might ask your learners to look at the best sellers in each book category on *Amazon*. What does this imply about U.S. culture? What does the ranking of certain items say? You might also have them check the kinds of gifts that people in the United States commonly give to each other, according to the Web site. Learners might note contrasts with their culture. They can also use such sites to check costs of certain items, read book excerpts, and check reviews (or add them) on texts read in class.

3. **Free E-card Sites**

   Students, especially those who do not draw well, can create and send beautiful electronic cards at *Blue Mountain* (http://www.bluemountain.com/), *Amazon*, or a number of other sites. Learners have choices among components; they have to use language to produce a message; and they learn about the format of cards, culturally appropriate greetings and messages, and holiday lingo. Plus, someone gets a card!

▶ Three New Technologies That Can Make a Difference

In other chapters, I have mentioned a variety of new and yet-undeveloped technologies that might change the way we teach and learn languages. The three that will have the most impact might be the following.

1. **Artificial Intelligence (AI)**

   Some experts say that true AI is yet to be invented, but each generation of computers is clearly able to simulate humans more closely. For language learning, computers in the near future could be able to respond creatively to learners, provide relevant feedback, and hold authentic conversations with learners. It will be interesting to see if our view of computers turns from tool to teacher with this revolutionary change.

2. **Self-Translating Software**

   Another tool under development is software that automatically and correctly translates documents into any language. Rudimentary examples of this technology are currently available both on the Web and in some software packages. If used effectively, when this tool finally trickles down to language classrooms it can help language learners to understand the nuances of translation between the first and second languages and to check their language against a model.

3. **Virtual Reality/Virtual Environments (VR)**

   Current VR applications include the ability to take a walk around a college campus or other site, travel through a computer, and explore the inside of a molecule. For language learners, VR environments could include such common language class settings as a grocery store, a restaurant, or a public bus, in which learners could explore and interact before actually leaving the classroom to experience the real environment.

▶ Three Fun But Not So Useful Things

Educators need to remember that pure fun once in a while is a great motivator, stress reducer, and community builder. For pure fun (and not a little incidental learning), I like to use the following:

1. **CrazyTalk**

   CrazyTalk (Version 3.5) allows users to make hilarious animations from any photo or facial image. Using this software's clever and simple interface, users can make anyone say (or sing!) anything, synchronized to movements of the mouth and other facial features. The images can be posted to the Web or shared through e-mail. Reallusion (http://www.reallusion.com/) has other packages that are just as much fun—check out their products.

2. **Simulation Games**

Sierra Entertainment (http://www.sierra.com/) has produced some logic games that students enjoy, such as King's Quest (Version 1.0). In them, the cartoon characters have to find and do things to reach the ultimate prize (such as freeing the princess). With virtually no text and a very compelling interface, these games are suitable for kindergarten and up. Teachers can integrate them into a multitude of language-based activities, from having students construct oral or written narratives as they work through the simulation to having them make an instructional manual to help others succeed at the game. A note of caution: Some of the simulations have risqué parts that would be inappropriate for learners.

3. **Web-Based Microworlds**

These interactive simulations, such as those at the *Secrets of Lost Empires* site (WGBH Science Unit, 2000), allow users to explore and to understand by doing.

▶ Three Most Important Guidelines For CALL Practice

Throughout this book, I have tried to emphasize these three guidelines. It is not always possible to follow them, but the results of doing so can make the use of technology a benefit, rather than a detriment, in CALL classrooms.

1. **Use it when you need to, not because it is there.**

This book has emphasized that computer technology, although it can support learning, should not be used just because it can be. Careful planning is important, as is using other technologies (books, overhead projectors, the chalkboard) when appropriate.

2. **Focus on language and content supported by technology, not on technology as an end itself.**

Instead of saying, or letting administrators say, "We have this technology, how can we use it?," educators need to think, "Here are my goals for content/language. Can technology help me in some important way to reach them?"

3. **Let learners teach you.**

Many of today's learners are growing up with computers and using them in ways that teachers might not have time or resources to study carefully.

By observing these students and helping them to serve as resources in classrooms, both learners and teachers can benefit.

▶ Conclusion

As educators plan to use technologies for language and content learning and teaching, they must continue to think critically about what they do in classrooms. Some educators still fear that technology can take the place of teachers; given the current state of technology, however, CALL professionals are correct in noting that effective and efficient use of technology must be planned by teachers. Nevertheless, in the future, new technologies may have the potential to function as a teacher, with the ability for creativity, responsivity, and initiative. Until that day, though, teachers in CALL classrooms should continue to think of ways that technologies can serve as tools to enrich language and content learning and provide more diverse and more authentic access to language data.

▶ Teachers' Voices

If we are going to let our kids search on the Internet, they need to know how to be discriminating. I have found that it is really hard to teach these skills—when applied to the Internet—to my fifth graders. So, I have found what is easiest for me is simply to preview the sites and let them search on just the few preapproved sites I give them. Maybe that is taking the easy way out, and I should try to do more with them on some of these skills. Internet use has been a toughie for me, because the majority of my kids struggle so much with reading anyway, and simply can't read much of what is on the Internet. There are some great graphics as well as some simpler sites that work, but I haven't yet found a way to allow them to search on their own.

As I was watching [a drama show on TV] the other night, one of the actors was at a wall screen (like our overhead wall screens), he would touch an image and another screen would pop-up with additional information. The other actors could view the information on the screen from the other side of the room. I was so excited and could imagine using something similar to this in the classroom. For example, in social studies we could review Brazil, touch the Amazon Basin, and view more information; touch a specific town on the

Amazon River and see even more information. How long will it be before this technology is in my room!

Technology use has certainly increased the self esteem of several of my ESL students. I think it is very empowering to be able to feel mastery over the use of some computer skills. There is a lot of pride involved. I have really enjoyed watching my students show their parents at conference time what they can do, and also watching how proud the parents are. It is pretty gratifying.—Now to just move that motivation to a few other subject areas.

References

Abilock, D. (1999). *NoodleTools 21st century literacies: Tools for reading the world*. Retrieved October 26, 2004, from http://www.noodletools.com/debbie/literacies/21c.html

Alderson, J. C., Clapham, C., & Wall, D. (1995). *Language test construction and evaluation*. New York: Cambridge University Press.

AlKahtani, S. (1999, November). Teaching ESL reading using computers. *The Internet TESL Journal*, 5(11). Retrieved September 9, 2004, from http://iteslj.org/Techniques/AlKahtani-ComputerReading/

American University. (2004). *Language and linguistics: TESOL*. Retrieved October 27, 2004, from http://www.library.american.edu/subject/language/tesol_t.html

Anderson, N. (2002). *The role of metacognition in second language teaching and learning*. (ERIC Digest). Washington, DC: ERIC Clearinghouse on Languages and Linguistics. (ERIC Document Reproduction Service No. ED463659)

Averill, J., Chambers, E., & Dantas-Whitney, M. (2000). Investing in people, not just flashy gadgets. In E. Hanson-Smith (Ed.), *Technology-enhanced learning environments* (pp. 85–98). Alexandria, VA: TESOL.

Avid Cinema (Version 1.0) [Computer software]. (1998). Tewksbury, MA: Avid Technology.

Backer, J. (2001, May). Using a modular approach to schMOOze with ESL/EFL students. *The Internet TESL Journal*, 7(5). Retrieved March 15, 2004, from http://iteslj.org/Lessons/Backer-SchMOOze.html

Barker, J. (2003). *Finding information on the Internet: A tutorial*. Retrieved March 31, 2004, from http://www.lib.berkeley.edu/TeachingLib/Guides/Internet/FindInfo.html

Basena, D., & Jamieson, J. (1996). CALL research in second language learning: 1990–1994. *CAELL Journal*, 7(1/2), 14–22.

Beare, K. (2003). *Speaking and listening lesson based on ordering food in a restaurant*. Retrieved September 20, 2004, from http://esl.about.com/library/lessons/blordering.htm

Bowe, F. (2000). *Universal design in education: Teaching non-traditional students*. Westport, CT: Bergin & Garvey.

Bowers, C. (1998). The paradox of technology: What's gained and lost? *Thought and Action, The NEA Higher Education Journal*, 14(1), 49–57.

Bradin, C. (1999). CALL issues: Instructional aspects of software evaluation. In J. Egbert, & E. Hunson-Smith (Eds.), *CALL environments: Research, practice, and critical issues*. Alexandria, VA: TESOL.

Brain Cogs (n.v.) [Computer software]. (2002). Watertown, MA: Fablevision. Available from http://www.fablevision.com/braincogs/index.html

Brown, H. (1994). *Teaching by principles: An interactive approach to language pedagogy.* Englewood Cliffs, NJ: Prentice Hall Regents.

Brown, J. D. (1997). Computers in language testing: Present research and some future directions. *Language Learning & Technology, 1*(1), 44–59. Retrieved March 31, 2004, from http://llt.msu.edu/vol1num1/brown/default.html

Burgstahler, S. (2002). *Universal design of instruction.* Retrieved May 14, 2004, from http://www.washington.edu/doit/Brochures/Academics/instruction.html

Burniske, R., & Monke, L. (2001). *Breaking down the digital walls: Learning to teach in a post-modem world.* Albany: State University of New York Press.

Byrd, P. (2001). *English grammar on the Web.* Retrieved October 27, 2004, from http://www.gsu.edu/~wwwesl/egw/index1.htm

Cammarata, L. (2003). *Which graphic organizers can I modify and print for use in my classroom?* Retrieved October 26, 2004, from http://www.tc.umn.edu/%7Eodax0004/EDITABLE.HTM

Carrell, P. (1987). Content and formal schemata in ESL reading. *TESOL Quarterly, 21,* 461–481.

Cary, S. (2000). *Working with second language learners: Answers to teachers' top ten questions.* Portsmouth, NH: Heinemann.

Chao, C. (1999). Theory and research: New emphases of assessment in the language learning classroom. In J. Egbert & E. Hanson-Smith (Eds.), *CALL environments: Research, practice, and critical issues* (pp. 243–256). Alexandria, VA: TESOL.

Chao, C. (2003). Professional development on cloud nine: Online conferencing. In J. Egbert (Ed.), *Becoming contributing professionals* (pp. 107–115). Alexandria, VA: TESOL.

Chapelle, C. (1998). Multimedia CALL: Lessons to be learned from research on instructed SLA. *Language Learning & Technology 2*(1), 22–34. Retrieved October 27, 2004, from http://llt.msu.edu/vol2num1/article1/index.html

Choices, Choices: Kids and the Environment (Version 1.0) [Computer software]. (1997). Watertown, MA: Tom Snyder Productions.

City University of New York. (2004). *TESLCA-L: Computer-assisted TESL-L branch of TESL-L list.* Available from http://www.lsoft.com/SCRIPTS/WL.EXE?SL1=TESLCA-L&H=CUNYVM.CUNY.EDU

Clare, M. (2000). *Internet essay exposer.* Retrieved October 26, 2004, from http://www.mattclare.ca/essay/

Cohee, L. (n.d.) *Wandering the world webquest.* Retrieved October 24, 2004 from http://www.plainfield.k12.in.us/hschool/webq/webq26/world.htm

Cohen, A. (2003). *Strategy training for second language learners.* Retrieved March 31, 2004, from http://www.cal.org/resources/digest/0302cohen.html

Connected Speech (Version 1.1) [Computer software]. (2001). Hurstbridge, Victoria, Australia: Protea Textware. Available from http://www.proteatextware.com.au/csna.htm

Connell, B., Jones, M., Mace, R., Mueller, J., Mullick, A., Ostroff, E., et al. (1997). The principles of universal design (Version 2.0). Retrieved March 31, 2004, from http://www.design.ncsu.edu:8120/cud/univ_design/principles/udprinciples.htm

Council for Exceptional Children. (1998). *A curriculum every student can use: Design principles for student access.* Retrieved March 31, 2004, from http://www.cec.sped.org/osep/ud-sec4.html

Crandall, J. (1994). *Content-centered language learning.* (ERIC Digest). (ERIC Document Reproduction Service No. ED367142). Retrieved March 30, 2004, from http://www.ericdigests.org/1994/content.htm

CrazyTalk (Version 3.5) [Computer software]. (2003). San Jose, CA: Reallusion.

Csikszentmihalyi, M. (1990). *Flow: The psychology of optimal experience.* New York: Harper & Row.

Csikszentmihalyi, M. (1997). Evolution and flow. *NAMTA Journal, 22*(2), 118–149.

Concordance. (Version 3.0). Available from http://www.rjcw.freeserve.co.uk/

Cuban, L. (2001). *Oversold and underused: Computers in classrooms 1980–2000.* Cambridge, MA: Harvard University Press.

Cultural Reporter (Version 1.0) [Computer software]. (1995). Watertown, MA: Tom Snyder Productions.

Cummins, J. (1999). *BICS and CALP.* Retrieved March 30, 2004, from http://www.iteachilearn.com /cummins/bicscalp.html

Dana, N., & Silva, D. (2003). *The reflective educator's guide to classroom research: Learning to teach and teaching to learn through practitioner inquiry.* Thousand Oaks, CA: Corwin.

Decisions, Decisions: The Environment (Version 2.0) [Computer software]. (1993). Watertown, MA: Tom Snyder Productions.

Diaz-Maggioli, G. (2003, August). *Professional development for language teachers.* Retrieved March 31, 2004, from http://www.cal.org/resources/digest/0303diaz.html

Director (Version 8.5) [Computer software]. (2001). San Francisco: Macromedia.

Discovery Communications. (2004). *The assassination of King Tut.* Retrieved October 26, 2004, from http://dsc.discovery.com/anthology/unsolvedhistory/kingtut/kingtut.html

Dodge, B. (1998). *The Webquest page.* Retrieved March 19, 2004, from http://webquest.sdsu.edu

Dragon Naturally Speaking (Version 7.3) [Computer software]. (2004). Marysville, CA: Dragon Naturally Speaking.

Dreamweaver. (Version 4.0) [Computer software]. (2001). San Francisco: Macromedia.

Duber, J. (2002). *CALL software reviews.* Retrieved October 27, 2004, from http://www-writing.berkeley.edu/chorus/call/reviews.html

Dunkel, P. (1999). *Considerations in developing and using computer-adaptive tests to assess second language proficiency.* (ERIC Digest). (ERIC Document Reproduction Service No. ED435202). Retrieved March 31, 2004, from http://www.ericfacility.net/ericdigests/ed435202.html

Dunkel, P. (n.d.). *Computer-adaptive testing of listening comprehension: A blueprint for CAT development.* Retrieved March 31, 2004, from http://www.sfli.bahcesehir.edu.tr/teacherpages/asim/papers /computer_adaptive.htm

East of the Web. (2002). *Wordgames.* Retrieved October 25, 2004, from http://www.eastoftheweb.com /games/index.html

Echevarria, J., & Graves, A. (2002). *Sheltered content instruction: Teaching students with diverse abilities.* Boston: Allyn & Bacon.

Eckstut, S. (1998). Focus on Grammar (Version Basic Level) [Computer software]. White Plains, NY: Addison Wesley Longman.

Egbert, J. (1994). Reading the Classifieds (n.v.) [Computer software]. Available from the CELIA Archive. Retrieved April 26, 2004, from ftp://ftp.latrobe.edu.au/pub/CELIA/

Egbert, J. (1995). Electronic action mazes: Tools for language learning. *CALL Journal, 6*(3), 9–12.

Egbert, J. (1999). Classroom practice: Practical assessments in the CALL classroom. In J. Egbert & E. Hanson-Smith (Eds.), *CALL environments: Research, practice, and critical issues* (pp. 257–271). Alexandria, VA: TESOL.

Egbert, J. (2001, May/June). Enhancing technology with external documents. *ESL Magazine, 14.*

Egbert, J. (2004). Access to knowledge: Implications of universal design for CALL environments. *CALL-EJ, 5*(2). Retrieved March 31, 2004, from http://www.clec.ritsumei.ac.jp/english/callejonline/8–2/egbert.html

Egbert, J., & Hanson-Smith, E. (1999). *CALL environments: Research, practice, and critical issues.* Alexandria, VA: TESOL.

Egbert, J., & Jessup, L. (2000). Systems analysis and design projects: Integrating communities and skills through the Web. In S. Gruber (Ed.), *Weaving a virtual Web: Practical approaches to new information technologies* (pp. 226–238). Urbana, IL: National Council of Teachers of English.

Egbert, J., & Petrie, G. (Eds.). (2005). *CALL research perspectives.* Mahwah, NJ: Lawrence Erlbaum.

Egbert, J., Yang, D., & Hogan, S. (2003, May). *CALL tasks for limited technology contexts.* Paper presented at WorldCALL 2003, Banff, Alberta, Canada.

ELLIS English Language Learning System (Version 3.0) [Computer software]. (2004). Rueil Malmaison, France: Formavision. Available from http://www.formavision.com/ellis/suite.htm

Encarta: The Complete Multimedia Encyclopedia (n.v.) [Computer software]. (1994). Redmond, WA: Microsoft.

EnchantedLearning.com. (2000). *Insects at Enchanted Learning.* Retrieved October 26, 2004, from http://www.enchantedlearning.com/themes/insects.shtml

Engle, M., & Cosgrave, T. (2004). *Critically analyzing information sources.* Retrieved October 26, 2004, from http://www.library.cornell.edu/okuref/research/skill26.htm

Ernst-Slavit, G., & Mulhern, M. (2003). Bilingual books: Promoting literacy and biliteracy in the second-language and mainstream classroom. *Reading Online, 7*(2). Retrieved March 15, 2004, from http://www.readingonline.org/articles/art_index.asp?HREF=ernst-slavit/index.html

ESL: Listening. (2004). Retrieved October 24, 2004, from http://iteslj.org/links/ESL/Listening/

ESL: Speaking. (2004). Retrieved October 24, 2004, from http://iteslj.org/links/ESL/Speaking/

Essential Teacher Tools (Version 1.2) [Computer software]. (2001). Watertown, MA: Tom Snyder Productions.

ETS. (2004). *TOEFL test preparation.* Available from http://www.ets.org/ell/testpreparation/toefl/index.html#free

Fisher, K. M., Becvar, L., Gomes, S. Levy, E., Noland, C., Smith, R., & Weeks, R. *Download SemNets.* Available from http://www.biologylessons.sdsu.edu/ta/about/semnetdown.html

Fizz and Martina's Math Adventure (Version 3.3) [Computer software]. (1999). Watertown, MA: Tom Snyder Productions.

Flash (Version 5.0) [Computer software]. (2000). San Francisco: Macromedia.

Florez, M. (1999*). Improving adult English language learners' speaking skills.* Retrieved September 20, 2004, from http://www.cal.org/ncle/digests/Speak.htm

Forcier, R., & Descy, D. (2002). *The computer as an educational tool: Productivity and problem solving* (3rd ed.). Upper Saddle River, NJ: Prentice-Hall.

Freeman, D., & Freeman, Y. (2000). *Teaching reading in multilingual classrooms.* Portsmouth, NH: Heinemann.

Freeman, Y., & Freeman, D. (1998). *ESL/EFL teaching: Principles for success.* Portsmouth, NH: Heinemann.

FrontPage (Version 4.0.2) [Computer software]. (1999). Redmond, WA: Microsoft.

Gardner, H. (1993). *Multiple intelligences: The theory in practice.* New York: BasicBooks.

Gibbons, P. (2002). *Scaffolding language, scaffolding learning: Teaching second language learners in the mainstream classroom.* Portsmouth, NH: Heinemann.

Glencoe/McGraw-Hill. (2004). *Internet safety and security: What teachers need to know. Teaching Today.* Retrieved October 26, 2004, from http://www.glencoe.com/sec/teachingtoday/educationupclose.phtml/39

Global SchoolNet Foundation. (2004a). *GeoGame: An interactive game for the Web.* Retrieved October 26, 2004, from http://www.gsn.org/GSH/project/gg/

Global SchoolNet Foundation. (2004b). *GeoGame project description.* Retrieved March 15, 2004, from http://www.gsn.org/GSH/project/gg/description.cfm

Goettsch, K. (2001). On-line journals: Creating community and competency in writing. In J. Burton and M. Carroll (Eds.), *Journal writing* (pp. 71–83). Alexandria, VA: TESOL.

Goodman, Y., Watson, D., & Burke, C. (1996). *Reading strategies: Focus on comprehension.* Katonah, NY: Richard C. Owen.

Gray, T. A. (n.d.). *How to search the Web: A guide to search tools.* Retrieved March 31, 2004, from http://daphne.palomar.edu/TGSEARCH/

Hall, P. (2001). *Are you what you eat?* Retrieved April 26, 2004, from http://www.manteno.k12.il.us/drussert/WebQuests/PaulaHall/Foods%20of%20the%20US.html

Hanford, M. (2002). Developing sociocultural competence in the ESL classroom. *Nottingham Linguistic Circular 17*, 1–16.

Harris, R. (2002, March). *Anti-plagiarism strategies for research papers.* Retrieved March 31, 2004, from http://www.virtualsalt.com/antiplag.htm

Healey, D. (2002). Interactive Web pages: Action mazes. In *Teaching and learning in the digital world.* Retrieved May 17, 2003, from http://oregonstate.edu/~healeyd/ups/actionmaze.html

Heater's World Productions. (1999). *AntBoy's bugworld!* Retrieved October 26, 2004, from http://www.heatersworld.com/bugworld/

Higgins, C. (1993). *Computer assisted language learning: Current programs and projects.* (ERIC Document Reproduction Service No. ED355835). Retrieved March 15, 2004, from http://www.ericfacility.net/databases/ERIC_Digests/ed355835.html

Holliday, L. (1999). Input, interaction, and CALL. In J. Egbert & E. Hanson-Smith (Eds.), *CALL environments: Research, practice, and critical issues* (pp. 181–188). Alexandria, VA: TESOL.

Holmes, M. (2002). *Action mazes.* Retrieved May 17, 2003, from http://www.englishlearner.com/llady/actmaze1.htm

Hooper, J., Medeiros, M., & Smith, D. (n.d.). *The steps of general inquiry & critical thinking.* Retrieved March 15, 2004, from http://www.educ.uvic.ca/faculty/sockenden/edb363/internetprojects/criticalthinking1/inquiry.html

Hot Potatoes (Version 6.0) [Computer software]. (2004). Victoria, British Columbia, Canada: Half-Baked Software. Available from http://web.uvic.ca/hrd/halfbaked/

Houghton Mifflin. (2001). *Project center: Movie in the making.* Retrieved October 26, 2004, from http://www.eduplace.com/projects/movie.html

Houghton Mifflin. (2004). *Education place project center.* Retrieved October 26, 2004, from http://www.eduplace.com/projects

HyperStudio (Version 3.0.) [Computer software]. (1995). Elgin, IL: Roger Wagner.

ICT4LT. (2001). *English home page.* Retrieved March 19, 2004, from http://www.ict4lt.org/en/index.htm

Imagination Express Destination: Time Trip USA (Version 1.1) [Computer software]. (1996). Novato, CA: Edmark.

iMovie (Version 3.0.3) [Computer software]. (2004). Cupertino, CA: Apple Computer.

Inquiry Page. (2001). *Inquiry page.* Retrieved March 15, 2004, from http://inquiry.uiuc.edu/

Inspiration (Version 6.0) [Computer software]. (2004). Portland, OR: Inspiration Software.

Interlink Language Centers. (n.d.) *On-line lessons: Reading skills.* Retrieved October 25, 2004, from http://www.eslus.com/LESSONS/READING/READ.HTM

International Association of Teachers of English as a Foreign Language. (2004). *Teaching English with technology.* Retrieved October 27, 2004, from http://www.iatefl.org.pl/call/callnl.htm

International Society for Technology in Education. (2000). *National education technology standards for students: Connecting curriculum and technology.* Eugene, OR: Author.

International Society for Technology in Education. (2002a). *Curriculum and content area standards.* Retrieved October 24, 2004, from http://cnets.iste.org/currstands/

International Society for Technology in Education. (2002b). *National educational technology standards for students.* Retrieved March 19, 2004, from http://cnets.iste.org/students/

Introduction to semantic networking. (n.d.) Retrieved October 26, 2004, from http://www.sci.sdsu.edu/BFS/first/semnet.html

Johns, T. (2000). *Data-driven learning page.* Retrieved October 25, 2004, from http://web.bham.ac.uk/johnstf/timconc.htm

Johnshoy, M. (2001). Search for a lesson or unit. In *CoBaLTT Web resource center.* Retrieved March 30, 2004, from http://carla.acad.umn.edu/cobaltt/lessonplans/search.html

Jung, H. (2003). *Language, literacy, and technology: A qualitative study of opportunities in technology-enhanced language learning (TELL) classrooms.* Unpublished doctoral dissertation, Washington State University, Pullman.

Kagan, S. (1994). *Cooperative learning.* San Clemente, CA: Kagan.

Kid Pix Studio Deluxe (Version 3.0 for Macintosh) [Computer software]. (1994–1996). Novato, CA: Broderbund Software.

Kidspiration (Version 2.0) [Computer software]. (2004). Portland, OR: Inspiration Software.

King's Quest (Version 1.0) [Computer software]. (1993). Bellevue, WA: Sierra Entertainment.

Kirsch, I., Jamieson, J., Taylor, C., & Eignor, D. (1998). *Computer familiarity among TOEFL examinees* (TOEFL Research Report 59). Princeton, NJ: Educational Testing Service.

Kitao, K., & Kitao, S. K. (1997). *Useful lists for linguistics and English.* Retrieved October 27, 2004, from http://ilc2.doshisha.ac.jp/users/kkitao/online/list/lis-ling.htm

Kreeft-Peyton, J. (Ed.). (1990). *Students and teachers writing together: Perspectives on journal writing.* Alexandria, VA: TESOL.

LaTrobe University. (2004). *Computer-enhanced language instruction archive.* Retrieved October 26, 2004, from http://www.latrobe.edu.au/education/celia/celia.html

Learning Point Associates. (1988). *Graphic organizers.* Retrieved October 26, 2004, from http://www.ncrel.org/sdrs/areas/issues/students/learning/lr1grorg.htm

Learning Point Associates. (1998). *The amazing picture machine.* Retrieved from http://www.ncrtec.org/picture.htm

Learning Point Associates. (2004a). *Learning with technology profile tool.* Available from http://www.ncrtec.org/capacity/profile/profwww.htm

Learning Point Associates. (2004b). *Professional development.* Retrieved October 26, 2004, from http://www.ncrel.org/info/pd/

Learning Point Associates. (2004c). *Technology professional development.* Retrieved October 26, 2004, http://www.ncrel.org/tech/tpd/index.html

Learning Point Associates. (2004d). *Using technology in PD.* Retrieved October 26, 2004, from North http://www.ncrel.org/pd/tech.htm

Levy, M. (1997). *CALL: Context and conceptualization*. Oxford, England: Oxford University Press.

Lightbown, P., & Spada, N. (2000). *How languages are learned* (Rev. ed.). Oxford, England: Oxford University Press.

LinguaSys Power Concordancer. (Version 2.0). Available as freeware from http://www.free-esl.com/all/call/software/details.asp?fIndex=6

Liu, M., Moore, Z., Graham, L., & Lee. S. (2003). A look at the research on computer-based technology use in second language learning: A review of the literature from 1990–2000. *Journal of Research on Technology in Education, 34*(3), 250–273.

Long, M. H. (1989). Task, group, and task-group interactions. *University of Hawaii working papers in ESL, 8*(2), 1–26.

Long, M. H. (1996). The role of the linguistic environment in second language acquisition. In W. C. Ritchie & T. K. Bhatia (Eds.), *Handbook of research on language acquisition. Vol. 2: Second language acquisition* (pp. 413–468). New York: Academic Press.

Macmillan Publishers (2004a). *Jazz chants: Listening skills for TESL and EFL*. Retrieved October 26, 2004, from http://www.onestopenglish.com/tefl_skills/listening_tefl_esl/jazzchant_preint.htm

Macmillan Publishers. (2004b). *The one stop magazine*. Retrieved October 26, 2004, from http://www.onestopenglish.com/news/index.htm

Macmillan Publishers. (2004c). *Speaking practice*. Retrieved October 26, 2004, from http://www.onestopenglish.com/tefl_skills/speaking.htm

Male, M. (1997). *Technology for inclusion* (3rd ed.). Boston: Allyn & Bacon.

Max's Toolbox (Version 1.5.1) [Computer software]. (2003). Adelaide, South Australia: eWord Technologies.

McCorduck, P. (1994). How we knew, how we know, how we will know. In C. L. Selfe & S. Hilligoss (Eds.), *Literacy and computers: The complications of teaching and learning with technology* (pp. 245–259). New York: Modern Language Association of America.

McCulloch, W. (2004). *Word surfing*. Retrieved October 27, 2004, from http://www.wordsurfing.co.uk/43682.html

McKenzie, J., & Bryce Davis, H. (1986). *From now on: Filling the toolbox*. Retrieved October 26, 2004, from http://www.fno.org/toolbox.html

Mercer Mayer's Just Me and My Mom (n.v.) [Computer software]. (1996). New York: GT Interactive Software.

Meyers, M. (1993). *Teaching to diversity: Teaching and learning in the multi-ethnic classroom*. Reading, MA: Addison-Wesley.

Mills, D., & Salzmann, A. (n.d.). *The grammar safari*. Retrieved October 26, 2004, from http://www.iei.uiuc.edu/web.pages/grammarsafari.html

Monoconc Pro (Version 2.2) [Computer software]. (2000). Houston, TX: Athelstan.

Murphey, T. (Series Ed.). (2003). *Professional development in language education series*. Alexandria, VA: TESOL.

Murray, D. (2000, September). Changing technologies, changing literacy communities? *Language Learning & Technology, 4*(2), 43–58.

National Academy of Sciences. (1996). *National science education standards*. Washington, DC: National Academy Press.

National Association for Music Education. (n.d.). *National standards for music education*. Retrieved March 30, 2004, from http://www.menc.org/publication/books/standards.htm

National Council for the Social Sciences. (1994). *Expectations of excellence: Curriculum standards for social studies.* Silver Spring, MD: Author.

National Council of Teachers of Mathematics. (1998). *Getting to know principles and standards.* Retrieved March 30, 2004, from http://www.nctm.org/standards/#annuals

National Geographic Society. (2003). *Crack the code.* Retrieved October 26, 2004, from http://www.nationalgeographic.com/xpeditions/activities/01/crackcode.html

National Geographic Society. (2004). *National geographic xpeditions: Geography standards in your classroom.* Retrieved October 26, 2004, from http://www.nationalgeographic.com/xpeditions/activities/matrix.html

National Inspirer (Version 1.0) [Computer software]. (1993). Watertown, MA: Tom Snyder Productions.

Neighborhood Map Machine (Version 2.0) [Computer software]. (2003). Watertown, MA: Tom Snyder Productions.

NoodleTools, Inc. (2004). *NoodleQuest – Search strategy wizard.* Retrieved October 27, 2004, from http://www.noodletools.com/noodlequest/

Northwest Regional Education Laboratory. (2001). 6+1 trait writing. In *Assessment.* Retrieved March 15, 2004, from http://www.nwrel.org/assessment/department.asp?d=1

Nyikos, M., & Hashimoto, R. (1997). Constructivist theory applied to collaboration: In search of ZPD. *Modern Language Journal, 81,* 506–517.

Ohio University. (2004). *Software reviews.* Retrieved October 27, 2004, from http://www.ohiou.edu/esl/teacher/technology/softReview.html

Online Safety Project. (2002). What are the risks? Retrieved March 24, 2004, from http://safekids.com/risks.htm

Opp-Beckman, L. (2003). *PIZZAZZ—People interested in zippy zany zcribbling!* Retrieved October 25, 2004, from http://www.uoregon.edu/~leslieob/pizzaz.html

Oppenheimer, T. (1997, July). The computer delusion. *The Atlantic Monthly, 280*(1), 45–62. Available from http://www.theatlantic.com/issues/97jul/computer.htm

The Oregon Trail (5th ed.) [Computer software]. Novato, CA: Broderbund Software.

Oxford, R. (1994). *Language learning strategies: An update.* (ERIC Digest). (ERIC Document Reproduction Service No. ED376707). Retrieved March 15, 2004, from http://www.ericfacility.net/databases/ERIC_Digests/ed376707.html

ParentOrganizer (n.v.) [Computer software]. (2001). Kirkland, WA: Parentorganizer.com.

Peregoy, S., & Boyle, O. (2001). *Reading, writing, and learning in ESL: A resource book for K–12 teachers* (3rd ed.). New York: Addison-Wesley Longman.

Pfaff-Harris, K. L. (n.d.). *Projects by students of English.* Retrieved from http://www.linguistic-funland.com/tesl-student-projects.html

Pica, T. (1994). Research on negotiation: What does it reveal about second-language learning conditions, processes, and outcomes? *Language Learning, 44*(3), 493–527.

Pickett, N., & Dodge, B. (2001). *Rubrics for Web lessons.* Retrieved March 31, 2004, from http://webquest.sdsu.edu/rubrics/weblessons.htm

Pinelli, T. E. (2004). *NASA scifiles instructional tools.* Retrieved October 26, 2004, from http://whyfiles.larc.nasa.gov/text/educators/tools/instructional.html

Postman, N. (1993). *Technopoly: The surrender of culture to technology.* New York: Vintage Books.

Purdue University. (2004). *English as a second language (ESL) resources, handouts and exercises.* Retrieved October 27, 2004, from http://owl.english.purdue.edu/handouts/esl/

Puzzle Power (Mac Version 1.0) [Computer Software]. (2000). Pinehurst, NC: Centron Software Technologies.

Qualifications and Curriculum Authority. (2001). *National curriculum in action: Geography.* Retrieved March 30, 2004, from http://www.ncaction.org.uk/subjects/geog/levels.htm

Quandary (Version 2.1) [Computer software]. (2004). Victoria, British Columbia, Canada: Half-Baked Software.

QuickTime (n.v.) [Computer software]. (2004). Cupertino, CA: Apple Computer. Available from http://www.apple.com/quicktime/download/

RealPlayer (n.v.) [Computer software]. (2004). Seattle, WA: RealNetworks. Available from http://www.real.com/player/?src=realaudio

Reader Rabbit: Dreamship Tales (Version 1.0) [Computer software]. (1994). Fremont, CA: The Learning Company.

Reading for Meaning (Version 1.0) [Computer software]. (2002). Watertown, MA: Tom Snyder Productions.

The Reading Matrix. (2003). *Second international online conference on second and foreign language teaching and research.* Retrieved October 27, 2004, from http://www.readingmatrix.com/onlineconference/

Reid, J. (Ed.). (1997). *Understanding learning styles in the ESL/EFL classroom.* White Plains, NY: Prentice Hall.

Richards, J., & Lockhart, C. (1994). *Reflective teaching in second language classrooms.* New York: Cambridge University Press.

Roman Catholic Diocese of Albany. (n.d.). *Internet safety/computer use policy for teachers and students.* Retrieved October 26, 2004, from http://www.rcdaschools.org/aup.htm

Rosenthal, J. (2003, January/February). Corpus linguistics: Discovering how we use language. *ESL Magazine,* 10–11.

Rosetta Stone (n.v.) [Computer software]. (2004). Harrisonburg, VA: Fairfield Language Technologies.

Ryan, K. (Ed.). (2000). *Recipes for wired teachers.* Available from http://jaltcall.org/books.html

Sammy's Science House (Version 1.4) [Computer software]. (n.d.). Novato, CA: Riverdeep Interactive Learning.

Schmidt, R. W. (2001). Attention. In P. Robinson (Ed.), *Cognition and second language instruction* (pp. 3–32). New York: Cambridge University Press.

SchoolMessenger USB (n.v.) [Computer software]. (n.d.). Scotts Valley, CA: Reliance Communications.

Schrock, K. (2003). *Kathy Schrock's guide for educators: Assessment and rubric information.* Retrieved March 31, 2004, from http://school.discovery.com/schrockguide/assess.html

Science Court: Work and Simple Machines (Version 1.0.3) [Computer software]. (1997). Watertown, MA: Tom Snyder Productions.

SemNet (n.v.) [Computer software]. (n.d.). San Diego, CA: San Diego State University College of Sciences. Available from http://www.biologylessons.sdsu.edu/ta/about/semnetdown.html

Setmajer-Chylinski, R. (2002). *Renata's ESL/CALL corner.* Retrieved October 26, 2004, from http://members.optushome.com.au/renatachylinski/4skills.htm

Short, D., & Echevarria, J. (1999). *The sheltered instruction observation protocol: A tool for teacher-researcher collaboration and professional development.* Retrieved March 30, 2004, from http://www.cal.org/resources/digest/sheltered.html

SimTown (n.v.) [Computer software]. (1995). Redwood City, CA: Maxis.

Smithsonian Institution. (2002). *Our story in history: Building a sod house.* Retrieved October 26, 2004, from http://americanhistory2.si.edu/ourstoryinhistory/tryonline/buildsodhouse.html

Spell-It Plus (n.v.) [Computer software]. (1989). Los Angeles: Davidson & Associates/Knowledge Adventure.

Sperling, D. (2004). *Dave's ESL café.* Retrieved October 25, 2004, from http://www.eslcafe.com/

Starter Paragraph Punch (Version 4.4) [Computer software]. (2004). New York: Merit Software.

Stevens, V. (1995). Concordancing with language learners: Why? When? What? *CAELL Journal, 6*(2), 2–10.

Straub, B. (1997). *Resources for teachers of basic skills.* Retrieved October 26, 2004, from http://www.humboldt1.com/~hope4all/

Strehorn, K. (2001). The application of universal instructional design to ESL teaching. *The Internet TESL Journal, 7*(3). Retrieved March 31, 2004, from http://iteslj.org/Techniques/Strehorn-UID.html

Swain, M. (1995, March). *Collaborative dialogue: Its contribution to second language learning.* Paper presented at the annual conference of the American Association for Applied Linguistics, Long Beach, CA.

Teachnology. (2003). *Project rubric generator.* Available from http://www.teach-nology.com/web_tools /rubrics/project/

TESOL. (1997). *ESL standards for pre-K–12 students.* Alexandria, VA: Author. Also available online from http://www.tesol.org/s_tesol/seccss.asp?CID=113&DID=1583

TESOL. (2003). *Standards for adult education ESL programs.* Alexandria, VA: Author. Also available online from http://www.tesol.org/s_tesol/seccss.asp?CID=364&DID=1981

Test of English as a Foreign Language (TOEFL) (n.v.) [Computer software]. (2005). Princeton, NJ: Educational Testing Service.

Thinkin' Things. (Version 3.0) [Computer software]. (2003). Novato, CA: Riverdeep Interactive Learning.

Tom Snyder Productions. (n.d.). *Cultural debates.* Retrieved October 26, 2004 from http://www.teachtsp2 .com/cdonline/

Turing, A. (1950). Computing machinery and intelligence. *Mind: A Quarterly Review of Psychology and Philosophy, 59*(236). Retrieved March 19, 2004, from http://www.abelard.org/turpap/turpap.htm

University at Buffalo. (2002). *Foreign language teaching forum.* Retrieved October 27, 2004, from http://listserv.buffalo.edu/archives/flteach.html

University of Maryland University College. (20043). *Copyright and fair use in the classroom, on the Internet, and on the World Wide Web.* Retrieved March 31, 2004, from http://www.umuc.edu/library /copy.html#copyright

University of Minnesota. (n.d.). *CoBaLTT instructional modules.* Retrieved October 26, 2004, from http://www.carla.umn.edu/cobaltt/modules/

Usborne's Animated First Thousand Words (n.v.) [Computer software]. (1997). Watertown, MA: Scholastic/Tom Snyder Productions.

Verizon. (2003). *Super thinkers.* Retrieved October 27, 2004, from http://www.enlightenme.com /enlightenme/superthinkers/pages/

Verizon. (2004a). *Enlighten me.* Retrieved October 27, 2994, from http://www.superpages.com /enlightenme/

Verizon. (2004b). *Internet learning tutor.* Retrieved October 27, 2004, from http://www.superpages.com /cgi-bin/php/ilt/index.html

Versatext Reading Development Program (Version 2.7) [Computer software]. (n.d.). Houston, TX: Novasoft/ICD/Athelstan.

Via Voice (Version 2.01) [Computer Software]. (2003). White Plains, NY: IBM.

VoxProxy (Version 2.0) [Computer software]. (n.d.). Golden, CO: Right Seat Software.

Warlick, D. (2003). *Pemission template.* Available from http://landmark-project.com/permission1.php

Warlick, D. (2004). *Citation machine.* Available from http://www.landmark-project.com/citation_machine /cm.php

Warschauer, M. (1996). Computer-assisted language learning: An introduction. In S. Fotos (Ed.), *Multimedia language teaching* (pp. 3–20). Tokyo: Logos International.

Warschauer, M. (1998). Interaction, negotiation, and computer-mediated learning. In V. Darleguy, A. Ding, & M. Svensson (Eds.), *Educational technology in language learning: Theoretical reflection and practial applications* (pp. 125–136). Lyon, France: National Institute of Applied Sciences, Center of Language Resources. Available from http://www.gse.uci.edu/markw/interaction.pdf

Warschauer, M. (2003, April). *Literacy and technology: Bridging the divide.* Paper presented at the Annual Meeting of the American Educational Research Association, Chicago, IL.

Watt, R. J. C. (2002). Concordance. (Version 3.0). [Computer software]. (2004). Dundee, Scotland: Author.

WGBH Science Unit. (2000). *Secrets of the lost empires.* Retrieved October 27, 2004, from http:// www.pbs.org/wgbh/nova/lostempires/

Who is Oscar Lake? (n.v.) [Computer software]. (1996). New York: Language Publications Interactive.

Widmayer, S., & Gray, H. (2002). *The sounds in "heed" and "hid."* Retrieved March 15, 2004, from http:// www.soundsofenglish.org/pronunciation/i.htm

Yahoo!. (2002). *Talk for free!* Available from http://messenger.yahoo.com/messenger/help/voicechat.html

Yahoo!. (2004). *How to search the Web.* Retrieved October 27, 2004 from http://dir.yahoo.com /Computers_and_Internet/Internet/World_Wide_Web/Searching_the_Web/How_to_Search_the_Web/

▶ Resources

▶ Print Resources

Basena, D., & Jamieson, J. (1997). Annotated bibliography of ESL CALL research: 1990–1994. *CAELL Journal, 7*(3), 12–18.

Boswood, T. (Ed.). (1997). *New ways of using computers in language teaching.* Alexandria, VA: TESOL.

Brinton, D., Goodwin, J., & Ranks, L. (1994). Helping language minority students read and write analytically: The journey into, through, and beyond. In F. Peitzman & G. Gadda (Eds.), *With different eyes: Insights into teaching language minority students across the disciplines* (pp. 57–88). New York: Longman.

Brinton, D., & Holten, C. (1997). Into, through, and beyond: A framework to develop content-based material. *Forum, 35*(4), 10–21.

Brinton, D., & Holten, C. (2001). Does the emperor have no clothes? A re-examination of grammar in content-based instruction. In J. Flowerdew & M. Peacock (Eds.), *Research perspectives on English for academic purposes* (pp. 239–251). Cambridge, England: Cambridge University Press.

Brinton, D., & Master, P. (Eds.). (1997). *New ways in content-based instruction.* Alexandria, VA: TESOL.

Brinton, D., Snow, M., & Wesche, M. (1989). *Content-based second language instruction.* Boston: Heinle & Heinle.

Brown, H. D. (2000). *Principles of language learning and teaching* (4th ed.). New York: Longman.

Cumming, A., & Berwick, R. (Eds.). (1996). *Validation in language testing.* Clevedon, England: Multilingual Matters.

Debski, R., & Levy, M. (Eds.). (1999). *World CALL: Global perspectives on computer-assisted language learning.* Lisse, Netherlands: Swets & Zeitlinger.

Dockterman, D. (Ed.). (1998). *Great teaching in the one-computer classroom* (5th ed.). Watertown, MA: Tom Snyder Productions.

Dunkel, P. (Ed.). (1991). *Computer-assisted language learning and testing: Research issues and practice.* New York: Newbury House.

Dunkel, P. (1999). *Considerations in developing and using computer-adaptive tests to assess second language proficiency.* (ERIC Digest). (ERIC Document Reproduction Service No. ED435202). Retrieved March 31, 2004, from http://www.ericfacility.net/ericdigests/ed435202.html

Ferneding, K. A. (2003). *Questioning technology: Electronic technologies and educational reform.* New York: Peter Lang.

Feyten, M., Macy, M., Ducher, J., Yoshii, M., Eunwook, P., Calandra, B., et al. (2002). *Teaching ESL/EFL with the Internet: Catching the wave.* Upper Saddle River, NJ: Pearson Education.

Gay, G., & Banks, J. A. (2000). *Culturally responsive teaching: Theory, research, & practice.* New York: Teachers College Press.

Gillette, S., Goettsh, K., Rowekamp, J., Salehi, N., & Tarone, E. (1999). *Connected: Using audio, video, and computer materials in the communicative classroom.* Minneapolis, MN: Master Communications Group.

Gonzalez-Lloret, M. (2003). Designing task-based CALL to promote interaction: En busca de emeraldas. *Language Learning & Technology, 7*(1), 86–104.

Grabe, M., & Grabe, C. (2004). *Integrating technology for meaningful learning* (4th ed.). New York: Houghton Mifflin.

Gruber, S. (Ed.). (2000). *Weaving a virtual web: Practical approaches to new information technologies.* Urbana, IL: National Council of Teachers of English.

Haley, M., & Austin, T. (2004). *Content-based second language teaching and learning.* Boston: Pearson Education.

Hochart, J. J. (1998). Improving listening and speaking skills in English through the use of authoring systems. *ReCALL, 10*(2), 18–24.

Hurley, S., & Tinajero, J. (2001). *Literacy assessment of second language learners.* Needham Heights, MA: Allyn & Bacon.

Irvine, J., Jones, J., Armento, B., Causey, V., & Frasher, R. (2000). *Culturally responsive teaching: Lesson planning for elementary and middle grades.* Boston: McGraw-Hill.

Kahn, J. (1998). *Ideas and strategies for the one-computer classroom.* Eugene, OR: International Society for Technology in Education.

Kasper, L. F. (1995). Theory and practice in content-based ESL reading instruction. *English for Specific Purposes, 14*(3), 223–230.

Kasper, L. F. (1997). The impact of content-based instructional programs on the academic progress of ESL students. *English for Specific Purposes, 16*(4), 309–320.

Kasper, L. F. (2000). *Content-based college ESL instruction.* Mahwah, NJ: Lawrence Erlbaum.

Khaine, M. S., & Fisher, D. (2003). *Technology-rich learning environments: A future perspective.* River Edge, NJ: World Scientific.

Meskill, G. (2002). *Teaching and learning in real time: Media, technologies and language acquisition.* Houston, TX: Athelstan.

O'Malley, J., & Pierce, L. (1996). *Authentic assessment for English language learners.* New York: Addison Wesley.

O'Riley, P. A. (2003). *Technology, culture, and socioeconomics: A rhizoanalysis of educational discourses.* New York: Peter Lang.

Peterson, S. (1999). *Teachers and technology: Understanding the teacher's perspective of technology.* San Francisco: International Scholars.

Quiñones, S., Kirshtein, R., & Loy, N. (1998). *An educator's guide to evaluating the use of technology in schools and classrooms.* Washington, DC: U.S. Department of Education.

Rigg, P., & Allen, V. (1989). *When they don't all speak English: Integrating the ESL student into the regular classroom.* Urbana, IL: National Council of Teachers of English.

Snow, M., & Brinton, M. (Eds.). (1997). *The content-based classroom: Perspectives on integrating language and content.* White Plains, NY: Addison Wesley Longman.

Swaffer, J. K., Romano, S., Markley, P., & Arens, K. (Eds.). (1998). *Language learning online: Theory and practice in the ESL and L2 computer classroom.* Austin, TX: Labyrinth.

Taylor, J., Jamieson, J., Eignor, D., & Kirsch, I. (1998). *The relationship between computer-familiarity and performance on computer-based TOEFL test tasks* (TOEFL Research Report #61). Princeton, NJ: Educational Testing Service.

Thompson, C. (2003, December 14). PowerPoint makes you dumb. *The New York Times*, p. 88.

Wainer, H. (Ed.). (1990). *Computerized adaptive testing: A primer.* Hillsdale, NJ: Lawrence Erlbaum.

Warschauer, M. (1998). Online learning in sociocultural context. *Anthropology & Education Quarterly, 29,* 68–88.

Warschauer, M. (1999). Introduction: Surveying the terrain of literacy. In M. Warschauer (Ed.), *Electronic literacies: Language, culture, and power in online education* (pp. 1–21). Mahwah, NJ: Lawrence Erlbaum.

▶ Software

Adiboo: Magical Playground (Version 2.13) [Computer software]. (2000). Torrance, CA: Knowledge Adventure.

The Amazing Writing Machine: Creative Writing & Drawing (n.v.) [Computer software]. (1996). Novato, CA: Broderbund Software.

Asia Inspirer (Version 4.0) [Computer software]. (1998). Watertown, MA: Tom Snyder Productions.

Authorware Working Model (Version for Macintosh) [Computer software]. (1993). San Francisco: Macromedia.

Beethoven, L. (1990). String quartet no. 14. The Vermeer Quartet (n.v.) [Computer software]. Burbank, CA: Warner New Media.

Between the Lines (n.v.) [Computer software]. (1996). Regina, Saskatchewan, Canada: Tyndal Stone Media.

Bilingual TimeLiner in English and Spanish (Version 4.0.2) [Computer software]. (1994). Watertown, MA: Tom Snyder Productions.

The Bilingual Writing Center: Spanish/English (School Version 1.02) [Computer software]. (1995). Fremont, CA: The Learning Company.

Blackmer, E., & Ferrier, L. (1994). Clear Speech Works (n.v.) [Computer software]. Elgin, IL: Sunburst Media.

Brahms, J. (1991). A German requiem, Op. 45 (n.v.) [Computer software]. Burbank, CA: Warner New Media.

Britten, B. (1991). The orchestra: The instruments revealed (n.v.) [Computer software]. Burbank, CA: Warner New Media.

California Academy of Sciences. (1992). LIFEmap Series (Organic Diversity, Animals With Backbones, Animals) (n.v.) [Computer software]. Burbank, CA: Warner New Media.

Classroom StoreWorks (Version 1.0) [Computer software]. (1997). Watertown, MA: Tom Snyder Productions.

Community Construction Kit (Version 1.2) [Computer software]. (1998). Watertown, MA: Tom Snyder Productions.

Connected Speech (n.v.) [Computer software]. (2001). Victoria, Australia: Protea Textware.

Creative Writer (n.v.) [Computer software]. (1994). Redmond, WA: Microsoft.

Desert Storm: The War in the Persian Gulf (n.v.) [Computer software]. (1991). Burbank, CA: Warner New Media.

Design Your Own Home Architecture (n.v.) [Computer software]. (1995). Eugene, OR: Abracadata.

Developing Critical Thinking Skills for Effective Reading (n.v.) [Computer software]. (2003). New York: Merit Software.

Disney's Animated StoryBook: Winnie the Pooh and the Honey Tree (n.v.) [Computer Software]. (n.d.). Burbank, CA: Disney.

English Language Institute. (2002). *Concordancing software* (n.v.) [Computer software]. Retrieved April 25, 2004, from http://www.eli.ubc.ca/teachers/resources/DDL_links/#Concordancing

English Practice (n.v.) [Computer software]. (2003). Toronto, Canada: Ray's Edusoft.

English Tutor for Windows (n.v.) [Computer software]. (n.d.) Cincinnati, OH: Exceller Software.

Escape From Planet Arizona: An EF Multimedia Language Game (n.v.) [Computer software]. (1997). Stockholm, Sweden: EF Education.

Essential: Math Worksheets (Version 1.2) [Computer Software]. (2001). Watertown, MA: Tom Snyder Productions.

Essential Teacher Tools (Version 1.2) [Computer software]. (2001). Watertown, MA: Tom Snyder Productions.

Essential: Word Worksheets (Version 1.2) [Computer Software]. (2001). Watertown, MA: Tom Snyder Productions.

Fizz and Marina's Math Adventures: Project Sphinx (Version 1.0) [Computer software]. (1999). Watertown, MA: Tom Snyder Productions.

Games in English. (Version Ages 4 & Up) [Computer software]. (1995). Cupertino, CA: Kidsoft.

Grade Machine (Version 6.9 for Macintosh) [Computer software]. (2000). Lynnwood, WA: Misty City Software.

Grammar for the Real World (Version 1.1) [Computer software]. (1999). Torrance, CA: Knowledge Adventure.

The Great Ocean Rescue (Version 2.0) [Computer software]. (1997). Watertown, MA: Tom Snyder Productions.

Hear Say (Version 2.7) [Computer software]. (2000). Bloomington, IN: Communication Disorders Technology.

How Computers Work: The Complex World of Computers Made Simple (n.v.) [Computer software]. (1993). Burbank, CA: Warner New Media.

The Intellitools Family. (n.v.) [Computer software]. (2004). Retrieved September 2, 2004, from http://www.inclusive.co.uk/others/intkeys.shtml.

Jump Start: 1st Grade (n.v.) [Computer software]. (1996). Glendale, CA: Knowledge Adventure.

Kid Riffs (n.v.) [Computer software]. (1995). Chantilly, VA: IBM.

Let's Visit Mexico (Version 3.0) [Computer software]. (1997). Fairfield, CT: Queue.

Live Action English: TPR on a Computer (n.v.) [Computer Software]. (2000). Berkeley, CA: Command Performance Language Institute.

Living Books: Green Eggs and Ham by Dr. Seuss (n.v.) [Computer software]. (1996). Novato, CA: Broderbund Software.

Math Mysteries: Whole Numbers (Version 1.0 for Macintosh) [Computer software]. (2000). Watertown, MA: Tom Snyder Productions.

Mayaquest Trail (Version 1.1) [Computer software]. (1995). Minneapolis, MN: MECC.

Mercer Mayer's Just Me and My Dad (Version Age 3+) [Computer software]. (1997). New York: GT Interactive Software.

Mighty Math: Number Heroes (Version 1.0) [Computer software]. (1996). Redmond, WA: Edmark.

Music Tracks (n.v.) [Computer software]. (1994). Escondido, CA: BeachWare.

The Other Side (Version 1.0) [Computer software]. (1999). Watertown, MA: Tom Snyder Productions.

The Print Shop Deluxe 20 (Version 12.0) [Computer software]. (2004). Novato, CA: Broderbund Software.

The Print Shop Essential (Version 12.0) [Computer software]. (2001). Novato, CA; Broderbund Software.

Pronunciation Power (Version 2.0) [Computer software]. (n.d.) Alberta, Canada: English Computerized Learning.

Quick View Plus (Version 8) [Computer software]. (2004). Chanhassen, MN: Avantstar.

Read On! Plus (Version 1.0) [Computer software]. (1998). Elgin, IL: Sunburst.

Road Adventures USA (Version 1.0) [Computer software]. (1999). Cambridge, MA: The Learning Company.

Science Court Series (Version 1.0.3) [Computer software]. (1997). Watertown, MA: Tom Snyder Productions.

Storybook Weaver Deluxe (Version 2.0) [Computer software]. (1996). Minneapolis, MN: MECC.

Talk Now! Learn American English (n.v.) [Computer software]. (1996). London: EuroTalk.

TESOL Quarterly–Digital: Volumes 1–30 [Computer software]. (2003). Alamosa, CO: Cybertech Enterprises.

That's a Fact Jack! Read: The Interactive Game Show to Review Literature (Version 1.0 for Macintosh) [Computer software]. (2000). Watertown, MA: Tom Snyder Productions.

The View From Earth (n.v.) [Computer software]. (1992). Burbank, CA: Warner New Media.

Virtual Language Center. (n.d.). VLC Edict Web Concordancer (English) (n.v.) [Computer software]. Available from http://www.edict.com.hk/concordance/WWWConcappE.htm

Vocabulary Companion (Version 1.0) [Computer software]. (1999). Eugene, OR: Visions Technology in Education.

Watt, R. (n.d.). The Web Concordances (n.v.) [Computer software and workbooks]. Available from http://www.dundee.ac.uk/english/wics/wics.htm

Where in the USA Is Carmen Sandiego? (Version for Macintosh) [Computer software]. (1996). Novato, CA: Broderbund Software.

Williams, R. (1992). King's Quest VI: Heir Today, Gone Tomorrow (Version 1.0) [Computer software]. Coarsegold, CA: Sierra On-Line.

Word Tales (Version Ages 4 to 7) [Computer software]. (1993). Burbank, CA: Time Warner Interactive Group.

Write On! Plus: Writing With Literature (Version 1.0) [Computer software]. (1997). Elgin, IL: Sunburst.

The Writing Trek (Volume 1.1) [Computer software]. (1997). Pleasantville, NY: Sunburst Technology.

The Yukon Trail (Version 1.0) [Computer software]. (1994). Minneapolis, MN: MECC.

▶ Videos

Apple Computer, the National Association for Bilingual Education, & TESOL (Producers). (1993). *Making connections: Learning, language, and technology* [Videotape]. Cupertino, CA: Apple Computer.

Northwest Educational Technology Consortium. (Producer). (1999). *Promising practices in K–12 videoconferencing* [Videotape]. Portland, OR: Author.

Northwest Educational Technology Consortium. (Producer). (2000a). *Global challenge at Columbia High: A world geography project* [Videotape]. Portland, OR: Author.

Northwest Educational Technology Consortium. (Producer). (2000b). *Harris Elementary travels the USA: A USA geography project* [Videotape]. Portland, OR: Author.

Northwest Educational Technology Consortium. (Producer). (2000c). *It's a wild ride at O'Leary Junior High: A math, science, language arts project* [Videotape]. Portland, OR: Author.

TESOL. (n.d.). Technology-mediated language learning and CALL videos. Available from www.tesol.org /pubs/catalog/tech.html

▶ Web-Based Resources

Akiko, W., & Nelson, B. (n.d.). *Student-produced multimedia projects: Pedagogy and practice.* Retrieved March 15, 2004, from http://langue.hyper.chubu.ac.jp/jalt/pub/tlt/97/dec/wakao.html

Bartoshesky, A., Gonglewski, M., & Meloni, C. (2002). Adapting and using Web-based foreign language resources. Paper presented at ACTFL 2002. Retrieved March 30, 2004, from http://www.nclrc.org /adapting.html

Beck, S. (1997). Evaluation criteria. In *The good, the bad & the ugly: Or, why it's a good idea to evaluate Web sources.* Retrieved April 25, 2004, from http://lib.nmsu.edu/instruction/evalcrit.html

Beggs, T. (n.d.). *Influences and barriers to the adoption of instructional technology.* Retrieved March 31, 2004, from http://www.mtsu.edu/~itconf/proceed00/beggs/beggs.htm

Bell, J. S. (1997, October). Introduction: Teacher research in second and foreign language education. *Canadian Modern Language Review, 54*(1). Retrieved March 31, 2004, from http:// www.utpjournals.com/product/cmlr/541/541-Bell.html

Bradin, C. B. (1999). *Selected bibliography for CALL.* Retrieved March 31, 2004, from http://edvista.com /claire/callbib.html

Brown University, The Education Alliance. (n.d.). Principles for culturally responsive teaching. In *Teaching diverse learners.* Retrieved March 30, 2004, from http://www.lab.brown.edu/tdl/tl-strategies/crt-principles.shtml

Brown University, The Education Alliance. (n.d.). The diversity kit: An introductory resource for social change in education. In *Teaching diverse learners.* Retrieved March 30, 2004, from http:// www.lab.brown.edu/tdl/diversitykit.shtml

Burkart, G., & Sheppard, K. (n.d.).*Content-ESL across the USA: A training packet.* Retrieved March 30, 2004, from http://www.ncela.gwu.edu/pubs/cal/contentesl/

Cable News Network. (2000) Grammar exercises. Retrieved April 26, 2004, from http://lc.byuh.edu /CNN_N/CNN-N.html

Calderon, M. E. (1999). *Promoting language proficiency and academic achievement through cooperation.* Retrieved March 15, 2004, from http://www.cal.org/ericcll/digest/cooperation.html

California State University. (1996). *CSU faculty development institute on distributed course delivery for problem based learning.* Retrieved March 15, 2004, from http://edweb.sdsu.edu/clrit/home.html

CALL@Hull. (2003). *CALL software database.* Retrieved April 26, 2004, from http://www.fredriley.org.uk/call/resources/swdb.htm

Camtech. (n.d.). *Word finder.* Retrieved April 26, 2004 from http://camtech2000.net/Pages/WordFind.html

Carolina TESOL. (2003). *ESL resources for mainstream teachers.* Retrieved March 30, 2004, from http://home.triad.rr.com/mythak/links/mainstre.html

Center for Applied Linguistics. (2003). *Selected references about research and practice of integrating language and content instruction.* Retrieved March 30, 2004, from www.cal.org/topics/ilc/ilcrefs.htm

Center for Applied Linguistics. (n.d.). *Integrated language and content publications and products.* Retrieved March 30, 2004, from http://www.cal.org/pubs/ilc_p.html

Chafe, A. (1999). *Computer mediated communication in the second language classroom.* Retrieved March 31, 2004, from http://www.stemnet.nf.ca/~achafe/commdlang_html.htm

Chamot, A. (1992). Learning and problem solving strategies of ESL students. *Bilingual Research Journal, 16*(3 & 4), 1–34. Retrieved April 25, 2004, from www.ncela.gwu.edu/pubs/nabe/brj/v16/16_34_chamot.pdf

Chapelle, C. (1997, July). CALL in the year 2000: Still in search of research paradigms? *Language Learning & Technology, 1*(1), 19–43. Retrieved March 31, 2004, from http://llt.msu.edu/vol1num1/chapelle/default.html

Chen, J. F. (1996). CALL is not a hammer and not every teaching problem is a nail! *The Internet TESL Journal, 2*(7). Retrieved March 31, 2004, from http://iteslj.org/Articles/Chen-CALL.html

Cintron, K. (1999). Teaching listening and speaking. In *Karin's ESL partyland.* Retrieved March 15, 2004, from http://www.eslpartyland.com/teachers/nov/listen.htm

CitySpeak English Language Instruction. (2003). *Taking control of the English language.* Retrieved March 15, 2004, from http://www.usingenglish.com/speaking-out/taking-control.html

Classroom teacher resources. (2004). Retrieved April 26, 2004, from http://www.mrshurleysesl.com/mainstreamteacher.html

Cochran, C. (n.d.). Grammar. In *Caroline's ESL Web site.* Retrieved April 26, 2004, from http://members.aol.com/Ccochran50/grammar.htm

Cochran, C. (n.d.). Reading. In *Caroline's ESL Web site.* Retrieved April 26, 2004, from http://members.aol.com/Ccochran50/reading.htm

Cohen, M. D., & Tellez, K. (1994). Implementing cooperative learning for language minority students. *Bilingual Research Journal, 18*(1&2), 1–19. Retrieved March 15, 2004, from www.ncela.gwu.edu/pubs/nabe/brj/v18/18_12_cohen.pdf

Contemporary Issues in Technology in Teacher Education. Available from http://www.citejournal.org/vol2/iss4/toc.cfm.

Conversation questions for ESL/EFL classrooms. (2002). *The Internet TESL Journal.* Retrieved March 15, 2004, from http://iteslj.org/questions/

Dana. N., & Silva, D. (n.d.). *Teacher inquiry defined.* Retrieved March 31, 2004, from http://www.coe.ufl.edu/courses/its/ddl/my%20downloads/inquiry/Chapter1.pdf

Darian, S. (2001). Adapting authentic materials for language teaching. *Forum, 39*(2). Retrieved March 30, 2004, from http://exchanges.state.gov/forum/vols/vol39/no2/p2.htm

Darling, C. (2003) Guide to grammar and writing. Retrieved April 26, 2004, from http://webster.commnet.edu/grammar/index.htm

Davis, R. S. (2004). General listening quizzes. In *Randall's ESL cyber listening lab*. Retrieved April 26, 2004, from http://www.esl-lab.com/index.htm

Denver Public Schools. (n.d.). *Integration ideas for the one computer classroom*. Retrieved April 26, 2004, from http://edtech.denver.k12.co.us/planner/idbank/ibonecmptr.htm

Dieu, B. (2003). Reading. In *The English department teachers' page*. Retrieved April 26, 2004, from http://members.tripod.com/the_english_dept/teachers.html#read

Duber, J. (2003). Cutting edge CALL demos. Retrieved April 26, 2004, from http://www-writing.berkeley.edu/chorus/call/cuttingedge.html

Eisenhower National Clearinghouse for Mathematics and Science Education. (2004). *Guidance for teachers*. Retrieved April 25, 2004, from http://www.enc.org/topics/inquiry/teach/

ESL listening. (2003). *The Internet TESL Journal*. Retrieved March 15, 2004, from http://iteslj.org/links/ESL/Listening/

ESL listening center. (2003). 1-language.com. Retrieved March 15, 2004, from http://www.1-language.com/esllistening/

ESL quizzes. (2003). 1-language.com. Retrieved April 26, 2004, from http://www.1-language.com/eslquizzes/index.htm

ESL: Student projects. (2004). *The Internet TESL Journal*. Retrieved April 23, 2004, from http://iteslj.org/links/ESL/Student_Projects/

Essberger, J. (2003a). *English grammar*. Retrieved April 26, 2004, from http://grammar.englishclub.com/index.html

Essberger, J. (2003b). *English reading*. Retrieved April 26, 2004, from http://reading.englishclub.com/

Essberger, J. (2003c). *English writing*. Retrieved April 26, 2004, from http://writing.englishclub.com/

FYI CareerKids. (2000). *The portfolio assessment kit: Elementary and secondary grades*. Retrieved April 23, 2004, from http://www.careerkids.com/1152x864/WPAK.html

Global SchoolNet Foundation. (2004). *CyberFair*. Retrieved April 23, 2004, from http://www.gsn.org/CF/index.html

Green River Community College. (n.d.). *Projects completed by GRCC-ESL students*. Retrieved April 23, 2004, from http://www.ivygreen.ctc.edu/avery/activities/projects/projects.htm

Gunn, C., Gordon, S., Lirette, C., & Lavelle, T. (n.d.). *Creative writing*. Retrieved April 26, 2004, from http://bogglesworld.com/creativewriting.htm

Hanson-Smith, E. (n.d.). *Technology in the classroom: Practice and promise in the 21st century*. Retrieved March 15, 2004, from http://www.tesol.org/s_tesol/sec_document.asp?TRACKID=&CID=298&DID=1064

Haynes, J. (2003). *EverythingESL*. Retrieved March 30, 2004, from http://everythingesl.net/

Healey, D. (1998). *CALL print resources*. Retrieved March 31, 2004, from http://ucs.orst.edu/~healeyd/gtesol/print_resources.html

Internet treasure hunts for ESL students. (n.d.) *The Internet TESL Journal*. Retrieved April 26, 2004, from http://iteslj.org/th/

INTIME. (2002). *Culturally responsive teaching*. Retrieved March 30, 2004, from http://www.intime.uni.edu/multiculture/curriculum/culture/Teaching.htm

Introduction to semantic networking. (n.d.) Retrieved October 26, 2004, from http://www.sci.sdsu.edu/BFS/first/semnet.html

Jason Foundation for Education. (2003). *The JASON project*. Retrieved April 25, 2004, from http://www.jasonproject.org/jason_project/jason_project.htm.

Jeffrey, D. M. (2003). Participation points system to encourage classroom communication. *The Internet TESL Journal, 9*(8). Retrieved March 15, 2004, from http://iteslj.org/Techniques/Jeffrey-PointsSystem .html

Johns, T. (1997). *Classroom concordancing/data-driven learning bibliography.* Retrieved April 25, 2004, from http://web.bham.ac.uk/johnstf/biblio.htm

Johnson, M. (1999, September). CALL and teacher education: Issues in course design. *CALL-EJ Online, 1*(2). Retrieved March 31, 2004, from http://www.clec.ritsumei.ac.jp/english/callejonline/4-2 /johnson.html

Journal of Research on Technology in Teacher Education. Information available from http://www.iste.org/jrte /about.cfm.

Kagan, S. (1995). *We can talk: Cooperative learning in the elementary ESL classroom.* Retrieved March 15, 2004, from http://www.cal.org/ericcll/digest/kagan001.html

Kavaliauskiene, G. (2002). A technique for practicing conditional sentences. *The Internet TESL Journal, 8*(3). Retrieved March 15, 2004, from http://iteslj.org/Techniques/Kavaliauskiene-Cond.html

Khuwaileh, A. (2000, July). Cultural barriers of language teaching: A case study of classroom cultural obstacles. *Computer Assisted Language Learning, 13*(3). Available from http://www.extenza-eps.com /extenza/contentviewing/viewJournalIssueTOC.do?issueId=640

Krajka, J. (2000). Using the Internet in ESL writing instruction. *The Internet TESL Journal, 6*(11). Retrieved March 15, 2004, from http://iteslj.org/Techniques/Krajka-WritingUsingNet.html

Kumar, V. S. (1994). *Computer-supported collaborative learning: Issues for research.* Retrieved March 15, 2004, from http://www.cs.usask.ca/grads/vsk719/academic/890/project2/project2.html

Lee, K. (2000). English teachers' barriers to the use of computer-assisted language learning. *The Internet TESL Journal, 6*(12). Retrieved March 31, 2004, from http://iteslj.org/Articles/Lee-CALLbarriers.html

Lesley University. (2004). *Evaluating Web sites.* Retrieved April 25, 2004, from http://www.lesley.edu /library/guides/research/evaluating_web.html

Liao, C. (1999). E-mailing to improve EFL learners' reading and writing abilities: Taiwan experience. *The Internet TESL Journal, 5*(3). Retrieved March 15, 2004, from http://iteslj.org/Articles/Liao-Emailing.html

Littlejohn, A., & Hicks, D. (2000). Problem solving. In *An A to Z of methodology.* Retrieved November 22, 2004, from http://uk.cambridge.org/elt/ces/methodology/problemsolving.htm

Madison Metropolitan School District. (1996). *Ideas for the one computer classroom.* Retrieved April 26, 2004, from http://danenet.wicip.org/mmsd-it/tlc/1comprm.html

Makers at Middlebury. (n.d.). *Makers' pages.* Retrieved April 23, 2004, from http://lang.swarthmore.edu /makers/index.htm

Markett, C. (n.d.). *"You can CALL me, CALL me anytime": ICT and second language learning.* Retrieved March 31, 2004, from http://www.cs.tcd.ie/Carina.Markett/docs/essayf.htm#_ftn1

McKenzie, W. (n.d.). *Ways of knowing: Multiple intelligences and instructional technology.* Retrieved March 31, 2004, from http://surfaquarium.com/im.htm

Menken, K., & Holmes, P. (2000, December). Ensuring English language learners' success: Balancing teacher quantity with quality. In *Framing effective practice: Topics and issues in education[,] English language learners.* Retrieved March 31, 2004, from http://www.ericdigests.org/2004–1/english.htm

Microsoft (2004). *Templates.* Retrieved April 23, 2004, from http://officeupdate.microsoft.com /templategallery/

Moras, S. (2001). Computer-assisted language learning (CALL) and the Internet. In *Karen's linguistics issues.* Retrieved March 31, 2004, from http://www3.telus.net/linguisticsissues/CALL.html

Morrison, S. (n.d.) Creating web-based language learning activities. CAL Resource Guides Online. ERIC Clearinghouse on Languages and Linguistics. Retrieved September 20, 2004, from http://www.cal.org /resources/faqs/RGOs/webcall.html

Moses, F. (2001). The structural drill in remedial teaching. *The Internet TESL Journal, 7*(7). Retrieved March 15, 2004, from http://iteslj.org/Techniques/Moses-Drill.html

Murphy, K., Richards, J., Lewis, C., & Garman, E. (2001). *Exploring best practices for using technology in a K–8 urban school: A practitioner faculty collaborative process.* Paper presented at the annual meeting of the American Educational Research Association, Seattle, WA. Retrieved March 31, 2004, from http:// www.wheelock.edu/pt3/Inquiry_paper.pdf

National Institute for Literacy. (n.d.). *Project-based learning and other on-line teaching resources.* Retrieved April 25, 2004, from http://www.nifl.gov/susanc/projbas.htm

New Mexico State University, College of Education. (2003). *Culturally responsive teaching.* Retrieved March 30, 2004, from http://mathstar.nmsu.edu/teacher/culture.html

Noijons, J. (1994, Fall). Testing computer assisted language testing: Toward a checklist for CALT. *CALICO Journal, 12*(1), 37–58. Retrieved March 31, 2004, from http://calico.org/journalarticles/Volume12 /vol12-1/Noijons.pdf

North Central Regional Educational Laboratory. (2003). *Critical issue: Using technology to support limited-English-proficient (LEP) students' learning experiences.* Retrieved April 26, 2004, from http:// www.ncrel.org/sdrs/areas/issues/methods/technlgy/te900.htm

Northwest Regional Educational Laboratory. (2001). *Culturally responsive teaching.* Retrieved March 30, 2004, from http://www.nwrel.org/cfc/frc/beyus10.html

Oklahoma State University. (n.d.). *Assistive technology.* Retrieved March 31, 2004, from http:// www.okstate.edu/ucs/stdis/web.html

Orwig, C. (2002). *Language learning principles.* Retrieved March 31, 2004, from http://www.sil.org /lingualinks/LANGUAGELEARNING/LanguageLearningPrinciples/Contents.htm

Paton, A. (1998). *The Internet: Why use the Internet and limitations.* Retrieved March 31, 2004, from http:// www.geocities.com/Athens/Agora/2609/internet3.htm#top

Patsula Media. (2004). *Listening lab.* In *ESLtown.com.* Retrieved March 15, 2004, from http:// www.patsula.com/esltown/listening/index.shtml

Penuel, W. R., & Means, B. (1999). *Observing classroom processes in project-based learning using multimedia: A tool for evaluators.* Presented at the Secretary's Conference on Educational Technology—1999, Washington, DC. Retrieved March 15, 2004, from http://www.ed.gov/rschstat/eval/tech/techconf99 /whitepapers/paper3.html

Platts, M. (n.d.). *Virtual CALL library.* Retrieved March 31, 2004, from http://www.sussex.ac.uk /languages/1-6-6.html

Professional development workshop resources. (2004). Retrieved April 26, 2004, from http:// www.tomsnyder.com/profdev/curriculum.asp

Rosen, L. (2002). *Teaching with the Web.* Retrieved March 15, 2004, from http://polyglot.lss.wisc.edu/lss /lang/teach.html

San Mateo County Office of Education. (2001). *Project-based learning with multimedia.* Retrieved April 25, 2004, from http://pblmm.k12.ca.us/topics_main.htm

San Mateo-Foster City School District. (n.d.). *Mr. patch's quilt club.* Retrieved April 23, 2004, from http:// www.smfc.k12.ca.us/technology/mrpatch/

Sasaki, Y. (1996). Classroom techniques for contextualization: How to make "this is a pen" a pragmatically motivated utterance. *The Internet TESL Journal, 2*(11). Retrieved March 15, 2004, from http:// iteslj.org/Techniques/Sasaki-Context.html

Sass, E. (2004). *Creativity/problem solving/critical thinking: Lesson plans and resources.* Retrieved April 25, 2004, from http://www.cloudnet.com/~edrbsass/edcreative.htm

Scholastic Book Company. (2003). *Tom Snyder Productions: Free stuff.* Retrieved April 23, 2004, from http://www.tomsnyder.com/free_stuff.asp

Schrock, K. (2003). *Kathy Schrock's guide for educators: Assessment and rubric information.* Retrieved March 31, 2004, from http://school.discovery.com/schrockguide/assess.html

Schrock, K. (2004). *Kathy Schrock's guide for educators.* Retrieved April 23, 2004, from http://school.discovery.com/schrockguide/

Self-study grammar quizzes. (2002). *The Internet TESL Journal.* Retrieved April 26, 2004, from http://a4esl.org/q/h/grammar.html

Soo, K. (2002). *Multimedia computer-assisted language learning (MCALL) project.* Retrieved March 31, 2004, from http://ezinfo.ucs.indiana.edu/~ksoo/proj.html

Spencer, S. A. (2003). Five minute lesson fillers. *The Internet TESL Journal, 9*(8). Retrieved March 15, 2004, from http://iteslj.org/Techniques/Spencer-5MinuteFillers.html

Sperling, D. (2003). *The ESL quiz center.* In *Dave's ESL café.* Retrieved April 26, 2004, from http://www.pacificnet.net/~sperling/quiz/

Starr, L. (2001). *ESL lessons for adult students.* Retrieved March 15, 2004, from http://www.education-world.com/a_tech/tech074.shtml

Stoller, F. L. (2002). *Content-based instruction: A shell for language teaching or a framework for strategic language and content learning?* Retrieved March 30, 2004, from http://www.carla.umn.edu/cobaltt/modules/strategies/stoller.html

Teaching K-8 (n.d.). *Teaching K–8 Magazine.* Retrieved April 23, 2004, from http://www.teachingk-8.com/frm/fs_technology.html?stamp=01512803242003

TESOL Computer-Assisted Language Learning Interest Section. (2003). *TESOL Computer-Assisted Language Learning Interest Section.* Retrieved March 31, 2004, from http://www.uoregon.edu/~call/index.html

TESOL Computer-Assisted Language Learning Interest Section. (2004). *ESOL Internet resources.* Retrieved April 23, 2004, from http://www.uoregon.edu/~call/cgi-bin/links/links.cgi?action=view_cat&category=15

Thorn, W. (1995). Points to consider when evaluating interactive multimedia. *The Internet TESL Journal, 2*(4). Retrieved March 15, 2004, from http://www.itdc.sbcss.k12.ca.us/curriculum/lessonplan.html

Turner, D. (2003). *Resources for ESL learners in mainstream classrooms and content-based ESL.* Retrieved March 30, 2004, from http://www.teslmanitoba.ca/contentlinks.html

2Learn.ca Education Society. (2004). *Project foundations @2learn.ca.* Retrieved April 25, 2004, from http://www.2learn.ca/Projects/projectcentre/projframea.html

University of Delaware. (2002). *Problem-based learning.* Retrieved March 15, 2004, from http://www.udel.edu/pbl/

University of Delaware. (n.d.). *Problem-based learning clearinghouse.* Retrieved April 25, 2004, from https://www.mis4.udel.edu/Pbl/

Vilmi, R. (1994). *Global communication through email: An ongoing experiment at Helsinki University of Technology.* Retrieved March 15, 2004, from http://www.ruthvilmi.net/hut/autumn93/global.html

Watson, K. L. (1999). WebQuests in the middle school curriculum: Promoting technological literacy in the classroom. *Meridian: A Middle School Computer Technologies Journal, 2*(2). Retrieved March 15, 2004, from http://www.ncsu.edu/meridian/jul99/webquest/index.html

Werff, J. (2003). Using pictures from magazines. *The Internet TESL Journal, 9*(7). Retrieved March 15, 2004, from http://iteslj.org/Techniques/Werff-Pictures.html

White, P. (2002). *Practitioner inquiry of a teacher's practice through autoethnography*. Paper presented at the annual meeting of the International Society for Cultural Research and Activity Theory, Amsterdam. Retrieved March 31, 2004, from http://www.psy.vu.nl/iscrat2002/white.pdf

Wong, P., & Williams, M. (1999). *Beyond drill and practice: Exploring IT tools for thinking*. Paper presented at the Educational Technology Conference, Singapore. Retrieved March 15, 2004, from http://www.moe.edu.sg/iteducation/edtech/papers/h7_1.pdf

Worcester, T. (1997). *Electronic portfolios*. Retrieved April 26, 2004, from http://www.essdack.org/port/

▶ Web Sites

Alaska Sea Grant College Program at the University of Alaska Fairbanks School of Fisheries and Ocean Sciences. (2004). *ARCTIC science journeys*. Retrieved September 20, 2004, from http://www.uaf.edu /seagrant/NewsMedia/MoreASJ.html

Association for Educational Communications and Technology (AECT). (2001). Retrieved October 25, 2004, from http://www.aect.org

Buck, G. (1999). *The English listening lounge*. Retrieved March 15, 2004, from http:// www.englishlistening.com/

Center for Applied Research in Educational Technology (CARET). (2004). Retrieved October 25, 2004, from http://caret.iste.org/

Chicago Public Radio. (n.d.). *This American life*. Retrieved April 26, 2004, from http://www.thislife.org

Cintron, K. (1999). *Karin's ESL partyland*. Retrieved October 24, 2004, from http:// www.eslpartyland.com/

Cochran, C. (n.d.) *Caroline's ESL Web site*. Retrieved October 24, 2004, from http://members.aol.com /Ccochran50/novaesl.htm

Computer Assisted Language Instruction Consortium (CALICO). (2004). Retrieved October 25, 2004, from http://www.calico.org/

Creative Technology. (2004). *Textoys*. Retrieved April 26, 2004 from http://www.cict.co.uk/software /textoys/index.htm

Davis, R. S. (2004). *Randall's ESL cyber listening lab*. http://www.esl-lab.com/index.htm

Dieu, B. (2004). *The English Department teacher's page*. Retrieved October 25, 2004, from http:// members.tripod.com/the_english_dept/teachers.html

The educator's reference desk. (n.d.). Retrieved April 26, 2004, from http://www.eduref.org/

English Daily. (2000). Retrieved March 15, 2004, from http://www.englishdaily626.com /conversation01.html

Epals.com classroom exchange. (2004). Retrieved April 26, 2004, from http://www.epals.com

esl-lounge.com. (2004). *ESL books guide: Teacher theory and practice*. Retrieved September 20, 2004, from http://esl-lounge.com/eslbooks.shtml

The ESLoop. (n.d.). Retrieved April 26, 2004, from http://tesol.net/esloop

ESL Sound. (2004). Retrieved April 26, 2004, from http://www.eslsound.com/index.htm

ESL teachers board. (n.d.). Retrieved April 26, 2004, from http://www.eslteachersboard.com

ESL webquests. (n.d.). Retrieved April 26, 2004, from http://www.call-esl.com/samplewebquests/ webquestcontents_htm.htm

Essberger, J. (2003). *The English club*. Retrieved October, 25, 2004, http://www.englishclub.com/

European Association for Computer Assisted Language Learning (EUROCALL). (2004). Retrieved October 25, 2004, from http://www.eurocall.org

Family Education Network. (2003). *Teachervision.com*. Retrieved April 23, 2004, from http://www.teachervision.com/

Florida State University. (2004). *Secret worlds: The universe within*. In *Molecular expressions: Science, optics, and you*. Retrieved April 26, 2004, from http://micro.magnet.fsu.edu/primer/java/scienceopticsu/powersof10/index.html

Global SchoolNet Foundation. (2004). *Global SchoolNet*. Retrieved April 26, 2004, from http://gsn.org/

Gunn, C., Gordon, S., Lirette, C., & Lavelle, T. (n.d.). *Boggle's world*. Retrieved April 26, 2004, from http://bogglesworld.com/

Guterba, L. (2003). *Kid info*. Retrieved April 26, 2004, from http://www.kidinfo.com/Young_children/Young_Children.html

Halderman, A. (n.d.). *English as a second language*. Retrieved April 26, 2004, from http://academic.cuesta.cc.ca.us/ahalderma/esl.htm

International Association for Language Learning Technology (IALLT). (n.d.). Retrieved October 25, 2004, from http://iall.net

Internet Talk Radio. (n.d.). *Museum.media.org*. Retrieved April 26, 2004, from http://museum.media.org/radio/

Krauss, M. (2004). *Listening page 1*. In *ESL independent study lab*. Retrieved April 26, 2004, from http://www.lclark.edu/~krauss/toppicks/listening.html

Li, R. (2002). *English as a second language*. Retrieved March 15, 2004, from http://www.rong-chang.com/

Liang, J., & Rice, S. (1999–2002). *FocusEnglish.com*. Retrieved March 15, 2004, from http://www.focusenglish.com/

Mighty Media. (2002). *International email classroom connections (IECC)*. Retrieved April 26, 2004, from http://www.iecc.org/

Mighty Media. (2004). *KeyPals club*. Retrieved April 26, 2004, from http://www.teaching.com/keypals/

National Center for Education Statistics. Arts review. In *The NCES students' classroom*. Retrieved April 26, 2004, from http://nces.ed.gov/NCESKids/CRUNCH/artreview.asp

1-language.com. (n.d.). Retrieved October 24, 2004, from http://www.1-language.com/

Oracle. (n.d.). *ThinkQuest library*. Retrieved April 26, 2004, from http://www.thinkquest.org/library/

Patsula Media. (2004). *ESLtown.com*. Retrieved October 25, 2004, from http://www.patsula.com/esltown/

Sheltered Instruction Observation Protocol (n.d.). Retrieved November 22, 2004, from http://www.siopinstitute.net

Stories1st.org. (2003). Sound. In *Stories1st.org*. Retrieved April 26, 2004, from http://www.1stperson.org/

TopCities.com. (2002). *Free Web pages for everyone*. Retrieved April 23, 2004, from http://www.topcities.com/

University College of the Fraser Valley. (1999). *ESL on-line listening/speaking*. Retrieved April 26, 2004, from http://www.ucfv.bc.ca/esl/dropspek.htm

University of Michigan School of Information. (2002). Reading zone. In *Kidspace@The Internet Public Library*. Retrieved April 26, 2004, from http://www.ipl.org/kidspace/browse/rzn0000

Index

T

 U

V

 W

Also Available From TESOL

CALL Environments: Research, Practice, and Critical Issues
Joy Egbert and Elizabeth Hanson-Smith, Editors

Content-Based Instruction in Higher Education Settings
JoAnn Crandall and Dorit Kaufman, Editors

Distance-Learning Programs
Lynn E. Henrichsen, Editor

ESL Standards for Pre-K–12 Students
TESOL

Internet for English Teaching
Mark Warschauer, Heidi Shetzer, and Christine Meloni

New Ways of Using Computers in Language Teaching
Tim Boswood, Editor

Standards for Adult Education ESL Programs
TESOL Task Force on Adult Education Program Standards

Teacher Education
Karen E. Johnson, Editor

Technology-Enhanced Learning Environments
Elizabeth Hanson-Smith, Editor

For more information, contact
Teachers of English to Speakers of Other Languages, Inc.
700 South Washington Street, Suite 200
Alexandria, Virginia 22314 USA
Tel 703-836-0774 • Fax 703-836-6447
publications@tesol.org • http://www.tesol.org/